E-Government Digital Frontiers - Transforming Public Administration through Technology

Edited by Kyeong Kang and Lifu Li

Published in London, United Kingdom

E-Government Digital Frontiers - Transforming Public Administration through Technology
http://dx.doi.org/10.5772/intechopen.1003429
Edited by Kyeong Kang and Lifu Li

Contributors
Aiga Balode, Ajith Asha, André Afonso Tavares, Appadurai Karthik, Arpan Subhashis Barik, Caroline Müller Bitencourt, Do Huu Hai, Ellen Wayenberg, Freddy Patricio Torres Briones, Ganesan Kannan, Ieva Bikava, Jaime Rodrigo, Karunakaran Zachariah, Kyeong Kang, Lifu Li, Lingyun Lan, Luis Eduardo Rengifo Aispur, Salazar Espinoza

First published in London, United Kingdom, 2025 by IntechOpen
IntechOpen is the global imprint of INTECHOPEN LIMITED, registered in England and Wales, registration number: 11086078, 167-169 Great Portland Street, London, W1W 5PF, United Kingdom

For EU product safety concerns: IN TECH d.o.o., Prolaz Marije Krucifikse Kozulić 3, 51000 Rijeka, Croatia, info@intechopen.com or visit our website at intechopen.com.

British Library Cataloguing-in-Publication Data
A catalogue record for this book is available from the British Library

E-Government Digital Frontiers - Transforming Public Administration through Technology
Edited by Kyeong Kang and Lifu Li
p. cm.
Print ISBN 978-1-83634-086-7
Online ISBN 978-1-83634-085-0
eBook (PDF) ISBN 978-1-83634-087-4

If disposing of this product, please recycle the paper responsibly.

Meet the editors

Dr. Kyeong Kang is an internationally recognised scholar in Computing Sciences at the University of Technology Sydney (UTS), where she earned her Ph.D.. She is a leading authority on the socio-technical and cultural studies of information systems. Dr. Kang has demonstrated leadership in research on digital service innovation and platform co-creation. She has led numerous high-impact publications and externally funded international research collaborations with academia and industry. Renowned for her excellence in integrating research and teaching, Dr. Kang has designed and led award-winning, research-led teaching projects that inspire emerging scholars. As a dedicated mentor, she plays a key role in shaping UTS's strategic research direction. Additionally, she has edited three academic volumes and contributed widely to global considerations on digital transformation and innovation.

Dr. Lifu Li's research mainly focuses on information systems, business analytics, live-streaming commerce, online entrepreneurship, and cultural studies. He is an Assistant Professor at the Faculty of Business, City University of Macau. His papers have been published in high-impact journals, such as *Computers in Human Behavior, Information Technology & People, International Journal of Human-Computer Interaction, Aslib Journal of Information Management*, and *Entrepreneurship Research Journal*.

Contents

Preface

The transformation of public administration through digital technologies is not only a trend but a profound shift reshaping institutional structures, governance models, and citizen-state interactions. This edited volume, *E-Government Digital Frontiers – Transforming Public Administration through Technology*, brings together a series of scholarly contributions that examine the multifaceted nature of digital transformation in the public sector. Through an interdisciplinary lens, it critically interrogates how technology is redefining the foundations of governance and public value creation.

The volume begins with foundational perspectives on digital governance, offering theoretical and conceptual insights that situate e-government within broader socio-technical and institutional contexts. These contributions are particularly relevant to public administration and political science scholars who seek to understand the underlying dynamics of administrative change in response to digital disruption.

The book then explores the design and delivery of user-centric digital services. These discussions are highly pertinent to researchers in human-computer interaction, service design, and information systems, offering practical and analytical insights into how inclusive, accessible, and responsive services can be developed through co-design and participatory methods.

Further chapters examine the integration of advanced technologies, such as artificial intelligence and automation, into public sector operations. These analyses value research communities focused on algorithmic governance, ethics in public policy, and emerging technologies, providing critical perspectives on institutional readiness, governance capacity, and the normative implications of machine-assisted decision-making.

Digital infrastructure and interoperability are addressed through detailed examinations of data governance, technical standards, and cross-sectoral collaboration. These chapters offer empirical and conceptual grounding for scholars and practitioners in systems integration, digital architecture, and information policy who are concerned with enabling scalable, secure, and cohesive public digital ecosystems.

Cybersecurity is another core theme, focusing on institutional risk management strategies and evolving policy frameworks. These chapters contribute to ongoing academic discussions within security studies, risk governance, and digital trust while offering guidance to practitioners responsible for safeguarding public digital assets.

The book also engages with the transformation of urban governance through innovative city initiatives and platform-based public service models. These contributions are directly relevant to scholars in urban studies, innovation management, and civic technology, as they illuminate how local administrations leverage digital infrastructure to co-create value, enhance sustainability, and improve quality of life.

Digital participation, data disclosure, and civic accountability address key issues related to open government and transparency. This content makes a significant contribution to democratic governance research, benefiting those studying open data ecosystems, civic engagement, and digital ethics.

Digital inclusion and equity are examined with a focus on addressing the structural barriers that limit access to digital services. These discussions advance debates in digital divide research, social policy, and equity-focused public administration, offering evidence-based insights into inclusive digital transformation strategies.

The book directs the institutional leadership and organisational capabilities required to sustain digital innovation in the public sector. These chapters hold value for scholars of change management, strategic leadership, and public sector innovation, offering conceptual frameworks and empirical reflections on institutional adaptability and resilience.

Overall, this volume provides a rich and comprehensive resource for a wide range of research communities, including—but not limited to—those in digital government, public administration, political science, information systems, policy studies, urban planning, and technology ethics. It bridges theory and practice, offering empirically grounded analyses and conceptual clarity that can inform future research, teaching, and policy development. By engaging critically with both the opportunities and limitations of e-government, this volume contributes to advancing an inclusive, accountable, and innovative public sector.

The editors sincerely thank all contributing authors for their intellectual thoroughness and commitment to scholarly excellence. We also acknowledge the valuable input of peer reviewers, whose feedback enhanced the coherence and academic depth of this collection. Special thanks go to the co-editor and editorial assistants, whose dedicated support helped ensure the timely completion of this volume.

Kyeong Kang
Faculty of Engineering and IT/SPPL,
University of Technology Sydney,
Sydney, Australia

Lifu Li
Faculty of Business,
City University of Macau,
Macau

Section 1

Digital Governance

Chapter 1

The Role of Government Support in Driving Online Entrepreneurship Development in the Post-Pandemic Era

Lifu Li and Kyeong Kang

Abstract

The integration of live streaming in e-commerce generates a convenient marketing environment and provides online entrepreneurs with opportunities to communicate with online consumers in real-time. The new online entrepreneurship established on live streaming platforms overcomes the shortcomings of the traditional entrepreneurial model and breaks the limitations of time and space. However, considering the diverse experiences and backgrounds of online entrepreneurs, blind policy support and financial assistance are not conducive to the sustainable development of online entrepreneurship. Based on the data analysis results, both platform support and policy support positively affect individuals' motivation for online entrepreneurship. Still, the relationship between cultural knowledge and online entrepreneurship motivation is insignificant. This requires scholars to understand the different impacts of various influencing factors and provide valuable suggestions for the governments and official departments. With the steady development of online entrepreneurship on live streaming platforms, the economic downturn, unemployment, and other problems caused by the epidemic will be solved gradually. Sustainable economic development in the post-pandemic era will be achieved gradually.

Keywords: online entrepreneurship, live streaming commerce, government support, post-pandemic era, ethnic minority group

1. Introduction

The online entrepreneurship discussed in the current study refers to new entrepreneurship that is promoted on live streaming platforms and based on the "e-commerce" + "live" mode [1]. Different from the traditional way of starting a business, online entrepreneurship is based on emerging technologies that enable real-time interaction between entrepreneurs and customers. With the popularity of video streaming technology, online entrepreneurs can market products and communicate with online consumers *via* live streaming channels, narrowing the emotional distance between online entrepreneurs and online consumers [2]. The distinct entrepreneurship mode lowers the threshold for entrepreneurship and overcomes problems, such as inconvenient transportation and a shortage of funds. Faced with the challenge of the post-pandemic era, the online entrepreneurship mode based on live streaming platforms can be a powerful model for economic recovery, promoting the live streaming market's strong potential and vitality [3]. This trend (online entrepreneurship based on the live streaming industry) has been expanding worldwide, with business companies and famous brands joining the scramble to engage online consumers. In China, the sales of live streaming commerce have been developing rapidly, with a yearly average growth of more than 150% [4]. For instance, during the Singles' Day shopping festival on the Taobao Live platform, a famous entrepreneur, Viya, successfully attracted 13 million online viewers, and related products were sold out in merely a few minutes [5]. Meanwhile, benefiting from the video streaming technology, the new entrepreneurship model builds an emotional connection between entrepreneurs and consumers, bringing a new form of marketing to the e-commerce industry [6]. Specifically, online entrepreneurs can recommend products *via* video streaming technology, interact with online consumers through the virtual gift-sending system, and display product information through the online store function. Hence, online entrepreneurship is the combination of Internet technology and real-time interactive practice.

Although existing scholars have identified the significance of online entrepreneurship established on live streaming platforms, few of them have discussed relevant challenges in live streaming industries and mentioned the importance of governments' support [7, 8]. Compared with traditional offline entrepreneurship, online entrepreneurship has no strict requirements for sites, human capital, working time, and funds. This is suitable for entrepreneurs who tend to transfer their innovative ideas into business but have limited financial resources. However, according to the Chinese entrepreneurship report presented by Ding et al., most online entrepreneurship cannot survive for more than 3 years [9]. Limited funding support and lack of entrepreneurial experience are the main reasons for failure. To resolve these challenges and encourage online entrepreneurs to build confidence, some policy support and entrepreneurship training are promoted by the government and official departments. For example, educational departments in China have designed various online training activities and built a new efficient model, named university-industry-government collaboration, aiming to guide entrepreneurs to avoid uncertain issues [10, 11]. Meanwhile, with the improvement of the FinTech ecosystem created by financial departments, younger entrepreneurs have more opportunities to receive online microloans [12]. In light of this, the first objective of this research is to discuss the role of governments' support in driving online entrepreneurship.

Furthermore, online entrepreneurs' backgrounds should be analysed while designing government support. Online entrepreneurs from different backgrounds, that is, age, gender, income level, and educational background, will have specific requirements for local governments. Specifically, for online entrepreneurs living in rural areas, financial grants and tax breaks can significantly decrease their financial pressure and boost their self-confidence [13]. For others from developed regions, the training in entrepreneurial capability will exert a more significant influence on their online entrepreneurship motivation [13]. In addition to focusing on online entrepreneurs' regional backgrounds, their gender, education, income, and even ethnic backgrounds could also affect their online entrepreneurship motivation on live streaming platforms [14, 15]. This requires local governments to understand their fundamental requirements and design suitable policies to support them. Without accurate research results, the effectiveness of government funding will be negatively affected. Thus, the second objective of this article is to discover how to design valuable official support.

The study can significantly contribute to the area of online entrepreneurship research. Although prior studies have explored the advantages of the combination of online entrepreneurship and video streaming technology, few of them have discussed its development in the post-pandemic era and mentioned the effect of government support. Hence, related findings can help governments and official departments understand the new trend of online entrepreneurship and focus on its impact on economic growth and social stability.

2. Literature review and hypotheses

2.1 Online entrepreneurship in post-pandemic era

The unprecedented epidemic of COVID-19 in 2020 resulted in a massive shock to the global economy. Facing the impact of the epidemic, entrepreneurship is an important measure to solve employment problems, drive economic growth, and promote social stability [16]. Influenced by the COVID-19 pandemic, online entrepreneurship has begun to change, and some new business modes, like live streaming shopping, distance education, and online office on telecommunication platforms, have become a trend globally [17]. The development of new entrepreneurial models is inseparable from the support of the government. Governmental support, as an essential opportunity, can significantly affect the online entrepreneurial environment, and it can be considered a positive predictor of individuals' entrepreneurial intentions. Based on the Capability-Opportunity-Motivation-Behaviour (COM-B) model, factors from the capability unit and the opportunity unit can significantly affect individuals' motivation, leading to their final behaviours [18]. This requires the governments to consider two aspects, including capability and opportunity, while supporting the development of online entrepreneurship. Firstly, specific training courses should be designed to improve individuals' entrepreneurial skills, enhancing their confidence in online entrepreneurship. Secondly, suitable policies should be designed by official departments, providing environmental opportunities for online entrepreneurs. Referring to the COM-B model, governments should focus on both macro and micro. An improved entrepreneurial ecosystem can not only attract individuals' entrepreneurial enthusiasm but also help societies regain economic vitality. As more and more people engage in online entrepreneurship on live streaming platforms, the unemployment problem in the post-pandemic era will gradually be resolved, and sustainable economic development will be achieved (**Figure 1**) [18].

2.2 Live streaming commerce

Due to the explosion of COVID-19 since 2020, more and more individuals have accepted the online shopping mode, and the number of live streaming commerce users has increased dramatically [19]. Because of the integration of live streaming in e-commerce, new opportunities are established to offer online customers a comfortable shopping environment based on a cyber-physical system [20]. The interactive mechanism created by live streaming platforms generates a convenient atmosphere for users to communicate with each other [21]. Live streaming commerce has achieved significant development worldwide and provided various opportunities to increase

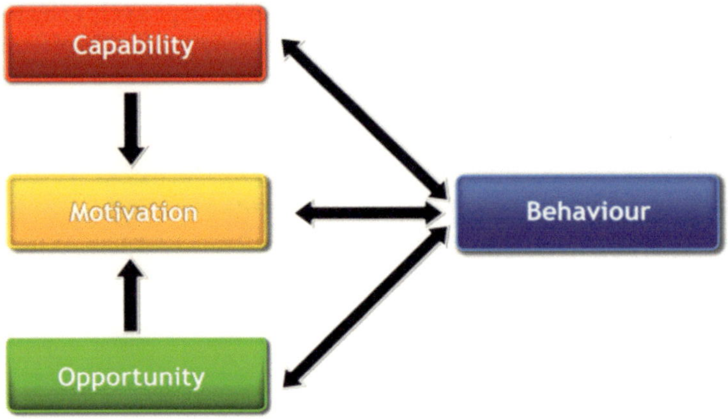

Figure 1.
The COM-B model [18].

communication, boost sales, attract attention, and win customers' trust. For example, Twitch, a popular live streaming platform around the world, has successfully attracted more than 9.52 million streamers and 2.95 million viewers [22]. In China, more than 50% of Chinese online users (approximately 617 million) have installed live streaming platforms and engaged in live streaming activities [22]. The rapid development of the live streaming industry not only brings social convenience to online users but also provides business opportunities for online entrepreneurs. Video streaming technology, as an essential tool, can assist online entrepreneurs in marketing and advertising, which is helpful in increasing online consumers' engagement and improving their shopping experiences [23]. Specifically, online entrepreneurs can use rich functions, like danmaku, virtual gift-sending, and online store functions, on the live streaming platform to promote products, attract customers, and increase sales. Online entrepreneurship built on live streaming platforms encompasses social, entertaining, and commercial, significantly disrupting the traditional business models. Considering its development prospects, governments and official departments tend to cooperate with live streaming platforms and provide online entrepreneurs with all kinds of assistance. This strategy can be helpful for online entrepreneurs to overcome potential challenges and promote online entrepreneurship successfully. In light of this, the related hypotheses are proposed as follows:

Hypothesis 1: Platform support positively affects online entrepreneurship motivation.

2.3 Support design based on entrepreneurs' backgrounds

Given the diverse experiences and backgrounds of online entrepreneurs, blind policy support and financial assistance are not conducive to the sustainable development of online entrepreneurship. To be specific, online entrepreneurs from remote areas face many difficulties, such as inconvenient transportation and economic backwardness, and they prefer to get fund-related assistance from official departments. Others from developed regions enjoy generous policy and economic support, and they tend to improve their capabilities and stand out internationally [24]. Policymakers should analyse online entrepreneurs' backgrounds and design specific policy support based on their requirements. In order to demonstrate the importance of adapting to local conditions, **Table 1** takes China's entrepreneurial background as an example

Comparison items	Developed areas in China	Developing areas in China
Younger entrepreneurs	Provide technical resources, funds, and entrepreneurship training	Share suggestions and guidance
Poor entrepreneurs	Build a comprehensive employment security system	Eliminate agricultural taxes
Ethnic minority entrepreneurs	Provide one-to-one vocational guidance	Lack of innovative training
Online entrepreneurs	Design "Internet Plus" university student innovation and entrepreneurship competitions. Provide venture guarantee loans (up to 2 million RMB)	Provide site rental and social insurance subsidies

Table 1.
The policy design comparison in China [25].

and compares the differences in policy setting between developed and less developed regions [25]. As **Table 1** shows, online entrepreneurs from developing regions can receive more financial support and mentoring from the local area compared to entrepreneurs from less developed regions. In light of this, entrepreneurs in different regions have specific advantages and challenges, and local governments should consider them comprehensively, design suitable policy support, and enhance individuals' entrepreneurial enthusiasm. Therefore, based on prior arguments, we propose that:

Hypothesis 2: Policy support positively affects online entrepreneurship motivation.

2.4 Ethnic minority group cultural knowledge

Similar to entrepreneurs' regional backgrounds, their particular gender, educational experiences, income level, and even ethnic backgrounds could also significantly impact their attitude towards online entrepreneurship, which official departments should focus on Refs. [26, 27]. In detail, online entrepreneurs from ethnic minority groups (EMGs) can not only get some labour and financial support but also receive cultural knowledge guidance from local communities [28, 29]. Prior studies have paid much attention to the typical entrepreneurs from the majority group, but few of them have focused on EMGs' online entrepreneurship motivation and identified their cultural advantages. Hence, the third influencing factor is designed based on EMGs' background, aiming to assist related scholars in understanding EMG entrepreneurs. Specifically, compared with the majority group entrepreneurs, online EMG entrepreneurs with cultural knowledge can transfer their cultural resources, like Thangka from the Zang group, food culture from the Hui group, and cheongsam from the Man group, to live streaming content and apply them to attract consumers' watching interests [30, 31]. Unique cultural resources can make EMG entrepreneurs stand out from their competitors, which existing literature has proved. This means that official departments should guide EMG entrepreneurs in taking advantage of their cultural resources and providing online consumers with cultural immersion experiences. The increasing participation of EMGs in online entrepreneurship not only promotes the steady development of the local economy but also plays an important role in preserving cultural diversity. Hence, EMG entrepreneurship should be supported by both the entrepreneurial sector and the cultural sector, and the article claims that:

Hypothesis 3: Cultural knowledge positively affects online entrepreneurship.

3. Methodology design

Based on the research objectives, the online questionnaire method can be applied to collect data samples and test the hypotheses. Compared with other surveying methods, the online questionnaire method has the advantage of focusing on different groups from different regions [32]. This study distributes online questionnaires among EMG entrepreneurs and utilises their replies as research samples. Because of the rapid development of online entrepreneurship in China, many EMGs have had abundant entrepreneurial experiences on live streaming platforms, which is helpful for the current study to understand their real opinions about online entrepreneurship. Meanwhile, the ethnic group categories in China are comprehensive, and 55 EMGs are officially certified by official departments. Unlike the EMGs from other countries, most Chinese EMGs have specific languages, writing systems, food culture, religions, and customs. Based on the improved online entrepreneurship environment and the comprehensive ethnic category in China, the EMGs' online entrepreneurship on Chinese live streaming platforms is chosen as the research context.

Moreover, all constructions measured in this study are based on previous scholars that are much related to the current study. For instance, policy support is examined through four questions from the social support research [33–35], and platform support is tested based on the technical platform research [36]. Cultural knowledge is evaluated based on prior cultural studies [37, 38]. Online entrepreneurship motivation is tested through three questions based on the entrepreneurial research designed by Lee-Ross [39]. The paper utilises the Likert 7-point scale with a range from the lowest score = 1 to the highest score = 7 to measure participants' answers [40].

Furthermore, online questionnaires were distributed among Chinese EMGs. To focus on the targeted group, some filtering questions have been added, such as participants' platform using experience, EMG background, and online entrepreneurship experience. One hundred fifty online questionnaires have been received from EMG participants. Among these 150 questionnaires, inappropriate responses have been deleted, including incomplete answers and mismatched ethnical backgrounds. Finally, 132 questionnaires were valid for this study.

4. Data analysis

4.1 Descriptive statistics

Regarding these 132 online questionnaires, 53.79% (71) of them are from male participants, and 46.21% (61) are from females. 40.15% (53) are between 26 and 40 years old, and 34.09% (45) are less than 26 years old (**Table 2**).

The variance-based structural equation modelling and partial least squares path modelling (PLS-SEM) have been utilised to promote data analysis and test the research model. The measurement model and structural model analysis are promoted through the SmartPLS 3.0. Applying the PLS-SEM analysis on the SmartPLS can explore the path coefficient and provide a deep understanding of the research model, which prior studies have identified [41, 42].

Demographic variables	Category	Frequency	Percentage (%)
Gender	Male	71	53.79
	Female	61	46.21
Age	≤25	45	34.09
	26–40	53	40.15
	≥41	34	25.76

Table 2.
The basic information of respondents (N = 132).

4.2 Measurement model and structural model

To evaluate the measurement model, reliability, convergent validity, and discriminant validity can be examined in the current study [43]. Firstly, the criteria, including AVE, composite reliability (CR), and Cronbach's Alpha, can be used to check the reliability of the research model [43, 44]. Specifically, AVE should be greater than 0.50, CR must be greater than 0.70, and Cronbach's Alpha needs to be greater than 0.70 [45]. As **Table 3** shows, all data results meet the requirements, indicating acceptable reliabilities.

According to the research developed by Chin (1998), convergent validity and discriminant validity can be tested based on confirmatory factor analysis. As the factor loadings and cross-loadings are presented in **Table 3**, the loadings in each construct are highly correlated, and each marked construct is higher than other constructs, meaning the convergent validity and discriminant validity of this research model are acceptable [46, 47]. In detail, according to **Table 3**, the range of marked items is

Item	Indicator	Out loading	Cronbach's Alpha	rho_A	Composite reliability	Average variance extracted (AVE)
Cultural knowledge	CU1	0.909	0.757	0.915	0.851	0.659
	CU2	0.708				
	CU3	0.805				
Online entrepreneurship motivation	ON1	0.881	0.833	0.834	0.900	0.750
	ON2	0.852				
	ON3	0.865				
Platform support	PL1	0.880	0.825	0.829	0.896	0.741
	PL2	0.868				
	PL3	0.835				
Policy support	PO1	0.880	0.825	0.825	0.895	0.741
	PO2	0.863				
	PO3	0.839				

Table 3.
The results of out loading, AVE, CR, and Cronbach's Alpha.

Item	CU	ON	PL	PO
CU	**0.811**			
ON	0.598	**0.866**		
PL	0.644	0.840	**0.861**	
PO	0.625	0.835	0.813	**0.861**

Bold: AVEs' square root.

Table 4.
Discriminant validity for the measurement model according to the Fornell-Larcker criterion.

Path	Original sample (O)	Sample mean (M)	Standard deviation (STDEV)	T-statistics (|O/STDEV|)	P values
CU - > ON	0.021	0.027	0.043	0.482	0.630
PL - > ON	0.468	0.470	0.081	5.799	0.000
PO - > ON	0.441	0.437	0.080	5.535	0.000

Table 5.
Hypothesis testing.

from 0.708 to 0.909, which is significantly higher than 0.707, meeting the convergent validity requirement [48].

In addition to the convergent validity, the discriminant validity can be tested by examining the Fornell-Larcker criterion. The AVEs' square root on the diagonal can assess whether the discriminant validity is acceptable [47, 49]. To be specific, the AVEs' square root on the diagonals in **Table 4** is significantly greater than other correlations, meeting the discriminant validity requirements.

According to data analysis results in **Table 5**, the relationship between platform support and online entrepreneurship motivation and the relationship between policy support and online entrepreneurship motivation can be supported because t-statistics results are notably higher than 1.96 [50]. Specifically, policy support has a significant positive effect on online entrepreneurship motivation ($\beta = 0.441$, $t = 5.535$, $p < 0.001$), and platform support also positively affects their online entrepreneurship motivation ($\beta = 0.468$, $t = 5.799$, $p < 0.001$), supporting H1 and H2. Meanwhile, the connection between cultural knowledge and online entrepreneurship motivation cannot be supported ($\beta = 0.021$, $t = 0.482$).

5. Discussion

5.1 Key findings and implications

Based on the data analysis results, platform support and policy support are two macro factors that positively affect individuals' motivation to promote online entrepreneurship on live streaming platforms. Considering the negative impact of the COVID-19 pandemic, the development of online entrepreneurship can effectively alleviate employment pressure and promote the steady recovery of the social economy. To drive the successful development of online entrepreneurship, related scholars and departments should consider the significant effects of platform support and policy support. Both of them can positively affect individuals' motivation for online entrepreneurship. Specifically, regarding platform support, platform managers and designers should improve the platform function design and build a more convenient entrepreneurial environment for EMGs. Regarding policy support, local governments and departments should clearly know EMG entrepreneurs' requirements and design specific entrepreneurial policies for them. Meanwhile, the relationship between cultural knowledge and online entrepreneurship motivation is insignificant. This could be because some EMGs lack a deep understanding of their cultural advantages and cannot apply cultural resources to streaming marketing processes. Related results should be focused on by the scholars. In future studies, it would be better if researchers could design an invitation letter and assist EMG participants in understanding the research topic and background. This method will be beneficial for participants in providing more accurate answers and improving the quality of the data analysis.

Regarding the implications of the current study, it aims to explain the effects of government support from two aspects. Firstly, it discusses the relationship between government support and online entrepreneurship development. Unlike traditional entrepreneurship modes, online entrepreneurship established on live streaming platforms has technical advantages and a flexible way of operating. With the help of online entrepreneurship advantages, the government can promote social and economic development, solve the employment problem, and achieve social stability in the post-epidemic era [51]. Due to some online entrepreneurs being unfamiliar with this new entrepreneurship model, governments should provide policy support and design training courses, assisting them in adapting to new business models on live streaming platforms. Various functions on live streaming platforms can not only reduce the difficulty of online entrepreneurship but also provide new ideas for advertising and marketing. Secondly, the government should understand online entrepreneurs' differences in background while designing specific official support. For instance, online entrepreneurs from remote areas face a backward economic environment and prefer to receive financial support and loan services. Others from ethnic and cultural backgrounds can apply their cultural advantages and transfer cultural resources to live streaming marketing content, making them stand out among competitors on live streaming platforms. The implementation of official support needs to consider the actual situation of entrepreneurs.

5.2 Limitations and future study

Although this article proposes the importance of the multi-group analysis based on entrepreneurs' gender, educational background, income level, and even ethnic backgrounds, future studies should consider the control variable design, aiming to provide accurate research results. Meanwhile, entrepreneurs from different countries, such as Eastern and Western countries, will also have unique opinions about promoting online entrepreneurship on live streaming platforms. Based on the Hofstede Cultural model, Eastern individuals pay much attention to collectivism and tend to cooperate with team members, and others from Western focus more on individualism [52]. The social and cultural differences require local governments to know their backgrounds and requirements while designing policy support.

6. Conclusion

Supporting online entrepreneurship plays a vital role in economic development and social stability, especially in the post-pandemic era. Online entrepreneurship established on live streaming platforms overcomes the drawbacks of the traditional model, such as space constraints, the number of personnel, and financial requirements. They provide individuals with new opportunities to promote e-business. Based on the data analysis results, both policy support and platform support can positively impact individuals' online entrepreneurship motivation. Considering the difficulties and challenges faced by online entrepreneurs, governments need to have a comprehensive understanding of their needs and help them build their entrepreneurial enthusiasm. With the steady development of online entrepreneurship, the economic downturn, unemployment, and other problems caused by the epidemic will be solved gradually. The recovery and steady improvement of economic performance will be achieved.

Author details

Lifu Li[1] and Kyeong Kang[2]*

1 Faculty of Business, City University of Macau, Macau

2 School of Professional Practice and Leadership, University of Technology Sydney, Australia

*Address all correspondence to: kyeong.kang@uts.edu.au

References

[1] Liu J, Zhang M. Formation mechanism of consumers' purchase intention in multimedia live platform: A case study of taobao live. Multimedia Tools and Applications. 2024;**83**(2):3657-3680

[2] Törhönen M et al. Streamers: The new wave of digital entrepreneurship? Extant corpus and research agenda. Electronic Commerce Research and Applications. 2021;**46**:101027

[3] Wu Z. Research on how live streaming helps revive the Chinese economy under COVID-19. In: SHS Web of Conferences. Les Ulis France: EDP Sciences; 2023

[4] Chen H, Dou Y, Xiao Y. Understanding the role of live streamers in live-streaming e-commerce. Electronic Commerce Research and Applications. 2023;**59**:101266

[5] Bu L, Xu L, Zipser D. The Innovations Behind China's Singles Day Shopping Phenomenon. Atlanta, United States: McKinsey & Company; 2019. pp. 1-4

[6] Li L, Kang K. Why ethnic minority groups' online-startups are booming in China's tight cultural ecosystem? Journal of Entrepreneurship in Emerging Economies. 2023;**15**(2):278-300

[7] Shou M, Yu J, Dai R. Identify the effect of government regulations on the live streaming e-commerce. Industrial Management & Data Systems. 2023;**123**(11):2909-2928

[8] Wang B et al. Evaluation of China's live streaming e-commerce industry policies based on a three-dimensional analysis framework. PLoS One. 2024;**19**(5):e0301451

[9] Ding N et al. Decision-making styles of Chinese business students. Journal of Education for Business. 2020;**95**(6):1-8

[10] Ding N et al. Decision-making styles of Chinese business students. Journal of Education for Business. 2019;**95**:351-358

[11] Sharif N, Tang HHH. New trends in innovation strategy at Chinese universities in Hong Kong and Shenzhen. International Journal of Technology Management. 2014;**65**(1-4):300-318

[12] Leong C et al. Nurturing a FinTech ecosystem: The case of a youth microloan startup in China. International Journal of Information Management. 2017;**37**(2):92-97

[13] Li L, Kang K. Impact of opportunity and capability on e-entrepreneurial motivation: A comparison of urban and rural perspectives. Journal of Entrepreneurship in Emerging Economies. 2022;**16**:932-953. (ahead-of-print)

[14] Barrera-Verdugo G et al. Influence of students' personality, gender, income and age on their intentions to create new information technology and telecommunications ventures. PLoS One. 2023;**18**(7):e0284488

[15] Paray ZA, Kumar S. Does entrepreneurship education influence entrepreneurial intention among students in HEI's? The role of age, gender and degree background. Journal of International Education in Business. 2020;**13**(1):55-72

[16] Zhang J, Huang J. Entrepreneurial self-efficacy mediates the impact of the post-pandemic entrepreneurship environment on college students' entrepreneurial intention. Frontiers in Psychology. 2021;**12**:643184

[17] Kit-fong A, Wenyue L, Zhaole L. The future of e-commerce: Live stream

shopping and purchase intention post-COVID-19. International Journal of Electronic Commerce Studies. 2022;**13**(3):147-184

[18] Michie S, Van Stralen MM, West R. The behaviour change wheel: A new method for characterising and designing behaviour change interventions. Implementation Science. 2011;**6**:1-12

[19] Yang J et al. Effects of interface design and live atmosphere on consumers' impulse-buying behaviour from the perspective of human–computer interaction. Sustainability. 2022;**14**(12):7110

[20] Sun Y et al. How live streaming influences purchase intentions in social commerce: An IT affordance perspective. Electronic Commerce Research and Applications. 2019;**37**:100886

[21] Kang K et al. The dynamic effect of interactivity on customer engagement behavior through tie strength: Evidence from live streaming commerce platforms. International Journal of Information Management. 2021;**56**:102251

[22] He D et al. Impacts of different interactions on viewers' sense of virtual community: An empirical study of live streaming platform. Behaviour & Information Technology. 2023;**42**(7):940-960

[23] Jiang Z et al. Propelling consumer engagement via entrepreneurs' live streaming? Frontiers in Psychology. 2022;**13**:890707

[24] He X. Digital entrepreneurship solution to rural poverty: Theory, practice and policy implications. Journal of Developmental Entrepreneurship. 2019;**24**(01):1950004

[25] Li L. Influencing Factors of the Online Start-Ups for Young Ethnic Minority Groups on the Live Social Platform. Australia: University of Technology Sydney; 2022

[26] Su Y, Li M. Applying technology acceptance model in online entrepreneurship education for new entrepreneurs. Frontiers in Psychology. 2021;**12**:713239

[27] Fanggidae RE, Nursiani NP, Angi YF. Women, entrepreneurs and online business (analysis of factors that motivate entrepreneurial women through online business). In: 3rd International Conference on Indonesian Social & Political Enquiries (ICISPE 2018). Dordrecht, The Netherlands: Atlantis Press; 2019

[28] Li L, Kang K. Ethnic minority group college students' liberal and conservative attitudes to online start-ups: Regional difference perspective. Journal of Entrepreneurship in Emerging Economies. 2023;**16**:1533-1554

[29] Li L, Kang K, Sohaib O. An analysis of cultural content on short video platforms: Cultural protection perspective. In: International Conference on E-Business and Telecommunications. Nanjing, China: Springer; 2021

[30] Li L. Impact of the propensity to cross-cultural adaptation on online viewers' attitudes toward ethnic minority group cultural streaming: An extension of the theory of planned behaviour. Computers in Human Behavior. 2024;**160**:108365

[31] Xie L. Comparative analysis of online and offline modes of thangkas selling. In: 2022 7th International Conference on Social Sciences and Economic Development (ICSSED 2022). Wuhan China: Atlantis Press; 2022

[32] Nayak M, Narayan K. Strengths and weakness of online surveys. IOSR Journal

of Humanities and Social Science. 2019;**24**(5):31-38

[33] Suurmeijer TP et al. The measurement of social support in the 'European research on incapacitating diseases and social support': The development of the social support questionnaire for transactions (SSQT). Social Science & Medicine. 1995;**40**(9):1221-1229

[34] Richman JM, Rosenfeld LB, Hardy CJ. The social support survey: A validation study of a clinical measure of the social support process. Research on Social Work Practice. 1993;**3**(3):288-311

[35] Abbasi MH, Siddiqi A, Azim RUA. Role of effective communications for enhancing leadership and entrepreneurial skills in university students. International Journal of Business and Social Science. 2011;**2**(10):242-250

[36] Balasubramanian K, Jaykumar V, Fukey LN. A study on "student preference towards the use of Edmodo as a learning platform to create responsible learning environment". Procedia-Social and Behavioral Sciences. 2014;**144**(1):416-422

[37] D'Agruma G, Hardy JT. Foreign languages and cross-cultural knowledge: A survey of their importance as perceived by human resources departments of Ohio's international businesses. Foreign Language Annals. 1997;**30**(1):38-48

[38] Mason JL. Cultural Competence Self-Assessment Questionnaire: A Manual for Users. Portland: Portland State University; 1995

[39] Lee-Ross D. An examination of the entrepreneurial intent of MBA students in Australia using the entrepreneurial intention questionnaire. Journal of Management Development. 2017;**36**:1180-1190

[40] Dawes J. Do data characteristics change according to the number of scale points used? An experiment using 5-point, 7-point and 10-point scales. International Journal of Market Research. 2008;**50**(1):61-104

[41] Sarstedt M, Cheah J-H. Partial least squares structural equation modeling using SmartPLS: A software review. Journal of Marketing Analytics. 2019;**7**(3):196-202

[42] Hair J et al. An updated and expanded assessment of PLS-SEM in information systems research. Industrial Management & Data Systems. 2017;**117**:442-458

[43] Hair JF et al. Multivariate Data Analysis. Vol. 5. Upper Saddle River, NJ: Prentice Hall; 1998

[44] Henseler J, Ringle CM, Sarstedt M. A new criterion for assessing discriminant validity in variance-based structural equation modeling. Journal of the Academy of Marketing Science. 2015;**43**(1):115-135

[45] Chin WW. Commentary: Issues and Opinion on Structural Equation Modeling. United States: University of Minnesota; 1998

[46] Clark LA, Watson D. Constructing Validity: Basic Issues in Objective Scale Development. United States: American Psychological Association; 2016

[47] Chin WW. Commentary: Issues and opinion on structural equation modeling. JSTOR. 1998;**22**:vii-xvi

[48] Hwang Y, Lee KC. Investigating the moderating role of uncertainty avoidance

cultural values on multidimensional online trust. Information & Management. 2012;**49**(3-4):171-176

[49] Fornell C, Larcker DF. Evaluating structural equation models with unobservable variables and measurement error. Journal of Marketing Research. 1981;**18**(1):39-50

[50] Hair JF Jr et al. A Primer on Partial Least Squares Structural Equation Modeling (PLS-SEM). United States of America: Sage Publications; 2016

[51] Shan B, Oh I, Rowley C. Innovation and Entrepreneurship in East Asia during the Digital Era: Post-Pandemic Prospects. London, U.K: Taylor & Francis; 2023. pp. 843-851

[52] Hofstede G. Dimensionalizing cultures: The Hofstede model in context. Online Readings in Psychology and Culture. 2011;**2**(1):8

Chapter 2

Evaluation of Public Policies and Interoperability from the Perspective of Digital Public Governance

André Afonso Tavares and Caroline Müller Bitencourt

Abstract

The present work is inserted in the field of public policies from an interdisciplinary analysis, beyond the exclusively legal one. The general objective was to understand the aspects of interoperability that could contribute to the process of evaluating public policies, since they optimize decision-making, creating a safer path for public action and realization of constitutional commitments through public policies. The research hypothesis was that technologies can promote public governance from the application of interoperability in order to result in the improvement of the public policy evaluation process, allowing greater monitoring, monitoring, rationalization of decision-making, and administrative action. The deductive method was used, and as a methodological approach, bibliographic research and consultation of legislative sources were used. It was found that interoperable action exponentially expands the application of techniques in programming and the use of more advanced technologies, in order to allow more dynamic, integrated, and timely assessments and thus support public managers in the mission of fulfilling constitutional objectives, in addition to being possible to apply it in different methods, by improving its techniques, reducing its costs, or reducing the time for its conclusion.

Keywords: digital public governance, evaluation of public policies, interoperability, public administration, public policy

1. Introduction

Evaluating the adequacy and sufficiency of the actions and services provided by public policy managers remains a challenge in the pursuit of good public administration. It is not that paradigms, methodological approaches, methods, and their instruments have not evolved over time and offered new horizons for evaluation, but rather that the isolation of external variables when verifying the results and impacts of public interventions still seems to be something that needs to be addressed or improved. The availability of information is not enough; it is necessary to organize and concatenate the data so that effective public transparency allows for monitoring, oversight, and evaluation of public policies. Evaluation requires parameters, guidelines, and planning in terms of the plan, instruments, actions, and execution. More than ever, planning is crucial.

The use of technology in the intricacies of public administration and in the way of interacting with managers, citizens, and businesses has resulted in what is conventionally referred to as digital government. Similarly, technologies in the context of public governance, that is, in the capacity to articulate and execute public interventions, have led to its derivation as digital public governance. However, these digital derivatives do not guarantee the modification of realities on their own. Along with this digital transformation, a new perspective on how to connect the involved actors is needed. Without this new vision, old bureaucracies are merely transferred to the digital realm without providing the enhancements that technologies have the potential to offer. Nonetheless, it must be kept in mind that technology serves a greater purpose, which is the realization of the objectives expressed by the Constitution. The commitment to fundamental rights, largely realized through public policies, was the chosen path for promoting greater social justice. The challenge is immense: advancing from the perspective of data and information operationalization, while maintaining commitment to the values of good public administration and fundamental rights.

Interoperability is one of the mechanisms that make up this new perspective that should accompany digital public governance, alongside other aspects such as openness, transparency, participation, and control, to produce a more democratic public administration focused on achieving constitutional objectives. In a scenario of extreme resource scarcity, the challenge of state efficiency in inclusive public management becomes an essential condition in public policies. It is not enough to have state action; precision, optimization, and results are necessary.

Thus, this research aims to address the following issue: how can interoperability applied in public governance contribute to the process of evaluating public policies, thereby optimizing the fulfillment of commitments made to the 1988 Constitution? The general objective will be to understand the aspects of interoperability that can contribute to the public policy evaluation process, as they optimize decision-making, creating a safer path for public action and the realization of constitutional commitments through public policies. The research hypothesis is that technologies can promote public governance through the application of interoperability, resulting in the improvement of the public policy evaluation process, allowing for better monitoring, oversight, rationalization of decision-making, and administrative action.

1.1 Method design

The deductive method will be used, with a methodological approach involving bibliographic research and consultation of legislative sources. The research will adopt an emphatically qualitative strategy, with analysis of regulations related to digital public governance and the operationalization of interoperability in the Brazilian public sector.

1.2 Research implications

The research has relevant theoretical and practical implications. In the theoretical field, it seeks to demonstrate how the evaluation of public policies, in a more advanced way, depends on a better structuring of digital public governance and the operationalization of interoperability. In the practical field, it demonstrates the difficulties of the process of evaluating public policies without an interoperability structure, as well as discussing practical reasons why, in the Brazilian context, there has been no progress in the issue of interoperability of computer systems and their databases.

1.3 Research structure

The work will be divided into two main parts. In the first, the use of interoperability in the context of digital public governance will be discussed. This will involve presenting the evolution of public governance, some differentiations, and the characteristics involving different models already conceived. Subsequently, interoperability, its dimensions, and the current treatment given by Brazilian legislation will be explained. In the second part, the previous concepts will be interwoven to reflect on the role of interoperability in the public policy evaluation process and understood here as a complex of decisions capable of enabling and realizing constitutional commitments. To this end, a review of different paradigms, methodological approaches, and methods of public policy evaluation will be conducted to understand their techniques, obstacles, and objectives. Finally, the aim is to understand how interoperability can contribute to the improvement of the public policy evaluation process, enabling efficient management understood as the ability to realize constitutional commitments.

2. Interoperability in digital public governance

It is understood that the process of evaluating public policies is closely related to how public governance is conceived. Just as the evaluation of public policies can vary according to the paradigm or underlying theory used, public governance will assume different forms and characteristics depending on the theory or approach utilized by those involved in performing public functions.

In this context, interoperability will have different conceptions or uses depending on the governance model established. Therefore, a review will be conducted on the various forms of public governance present in the scientific literature, with a focus on the Brazilian reality, as well as an analysis of the doctrinal and legal provisions related to interoperability, including recent legislative innovations.

2.1 Public governance in Brazil

To understand how interoperability connects to the theme of public governance, it is necessary to review the main concepts of governance in the public sector present in the scientific literature, as the differences between them also impact the ability to act interoperably.

Before delving into this, it is important to distinguish other terms that commonly appear together and, although they relate to and may influence each other, emphasizing or hindering their own characteristics, do not represent semantic equivalence: public administration, public management, governability, and public governance.

This differentiation is necessary because digital transformation in public administration, as described by Covas [1], brings significant changes not only in structure but also in process and procedure. This transformation involves more than just government and governance; the "conventional logic of the state-administration boundary" is less relevant than the discussion about open governability, allied with the emergence of smart cities and collaborative platforms.

In simpler terms, public administration can be understood as a "synonym for state organization," while public management is the "process of managing this organization". Research on public administration aims to study its structure, "the differences between its strategic core, its exclusive and non-exclusive activities, its level of professionalization, its effectiveness in enforcing laws and public policies," and the relationships between public servants and other actors. Conversely, research on public management focuses on "administrative strategies, mainly result-oriented management and excellence in competency" [2].

Bresser-Pereira [3] further distinguishes governability from governance. According to the author, governability refers to the "capacity to govern derived from the legitimacy of the state and its government with civil society," while governance is the "capacity for financial/managerial formulation and implementation of public policies." Governability is the capacity to solve social issues through the creation of public policies, associated with the exercise of power. Governance, on the other hand, is associated with the state's ability to act [4]. Additionally, the notion of governability may include the notion of environment, i.e., the capacity of the ruler to obtain an environment or conditions conducive to the exercise of their government.

In this vein, Húngaro [5] emphasizes that governability can also be understood as "the power of the state to govern, given its democratic legitimacy and the support it has in civil society," as well as being related to the "ability to ensure systemic and institutional conditions for the organization to fulfill its mission, intermediating the balance of interests among various stakeholders." Public governance can be understood as a "system that ensures stakeholders the strategic governance of public organizations and effective monitoring of senior management."

Public governance differs from public management in that the former concerns the quality of the decision-making process and its effectiveness, i.e., it directs, evaluates, and monitors management, while the latter receives superior direction and focuses on the quality of implementing this direction, with effectiveness and efficiency, i.e., it plans, executes, and controls [6].

García [7] notes that the concept of governance is subject to influences from transformations experienced by societies, driven by economic or political conceptions, from a more reductionist view of the state's role to a more cooperative or directive perspective. Thus, more than the concept itself, it is necessary to understand the characteristics of public governance to ascertain which elements of each model are present and whether a pure format can be found in Brazilian public governance.

Before delving into the analysis of Brazilian public governance, it is important to note that García [7] distinguishes three main arrangements of public governance when analyzed from the perspective of responsibility and authority and considering citizen participation instruments: hierarchical or traditional; corporate or market-based; and network or interactive. In hierarchical or traditional governance, the state plays a fundamental role in social coordination through political and institutional authority. Citizen participation mechanisms are primarily electoral or sectoral, segmented in some public policies requiring additional legitimacy. In corporate or market-based governance, public managers act as mediators or articulators of different interests and social values. This system prioritizes efficiency and economic rationality, with the market playing a fundamental role in social coordination through voluntary exchange. Citizen participation, therefore, is subordinate to prevailing economic interests in the market. Lastly, in network or interactive governance, the aim is to reflect the complexity, diversity, and heterogeneity of actors, their interests, rules, and values in contemporary societies. It seeks to combine elements of representative liberal democracy with those strengthening community participation and deliberation mechanisms. Thus, social coordination involves resolving social problems through the coordination of interactions among stakeholders.

This differentiation is important because depending on the modulation of public governance based on a certain conception, its mechanisms, including interoperability, will be affected. Therefore, interoperability can take different forms depending on the background conception of public governance.

Once these conceptual and characteristic differentiations are surpassed, the evolution of the idea of public governance in the Brazilian context is examined. It should be noted that the first concepts of governance began in the private sector in 1932, with its appearance in the public sector occurring later, in the early 1990s, during a historical context marked by financial crises [8]. During this time, Húngaro [5] details that the concept of public governance began to be used in discussions within international committees, introduced by the United Nations (UN), the United Nations Development Programme (UNDP), the Organization for Economic Co-operation and Development (OECD), the World Bank, the International Monetary Fund (IMF), and European organizations, linking it to deregulation, transparency, and accountability of public agents.

In Brazil, with the State Apparatus Reform Plan in 1995 and the promulgation of Constitutional Amendment No. 19 in 1998, a managerial reform of public administration was implemented, introducing the concept of public governance.

It is thus evident that the Brazilian public governance model present until then, although there was no explicit concern, was largely associated with the traditional and hierarchical governance model due to the established bureaucratic public administration model, with some elements of participation or deliberation by civil society, reflecting network or interactive governance.

It should be noted that the Brazilian Constitution promulgated in 1988 made it necessary to adjust the government structure to ensure the range of social rights outlined, especially through public policies. However, in the 1990s, when a new political and fiscal regime was introduced in Brazilian public administration, the government structure was redesigned according to what became known as new public management (NPM). This reform of public administration, in turn, also impacted the public governance model, seeking to include elements of corporate or market governance. However, this market-driven public governance, as with its implementation in other countries influenced by this thought, in Brazil, despite some improvements, still predominantly reflects the traditional governance conception.

At this point, regarding the Brazilian public administration reform of the 1990s, it is important to highlight that there was a mismatch between the objectives established by the 1988 Constitution, especially regarding the realization of fundamental and social rights. On one hand, the NPM model advocated for a subsidiary state or public administration, while the 1988 Constitution envisioned a strong and directly active social state fulfilling its commitments.

Finally, regarding the legal evolution of public governance in Brazil, on February 23, 2005, Decree No. 5378 was published, establishing the National Public Management and Deregulation Program—Gespública, which aimed to "contribute to improving the quality of public services provided to citizens and increasing the country's competitiveness." The decree anticipated the participation of individuals and organizations, both public and private, in Gespública actions, with express provisions in its steering committee, according to Article 8, item III, for representatives of private entities notably engaged in actions related to management quality and deregulation, through an act of the Minister of Planning, Budget, and Management [9].

Decree No. 9203, of November 22, 2017, revoked Decree No. 5378/2005 and addressed, at the federal level, the public administration governance policy. It also brought a legal concept of public governance in Article 2, item I, i.e., the "set of leadership, strategy, and control mechanisms put in place to evaluate, guide, and monitor management, with a view to conducting public policies and providing services in the interest of society," and established, in Article 3, principles such as responsiveness, integrity, reliability, regulatory improvement, accountability, and transparency [10].

It is noteworthy that although the aforementioned Decree included one of its guidelines, in Article 4, for decision-making oriented by support for societal participation, it did not create any instruments or details on how participation should be considered in public decisions or how society would effectively integrate into public governance, limiting participation to the establishment of specific working groups, according to Article 10-A, where private entities may be invited by the Interministerial Governance Committee (CIG).

It is worth noting that, through Constitutional Amendment No. 108, of August 26, 2020, which added a sole paragraph to Article 193 of the Constitution of the Federative Republic of Brazil, addressing the social order, social participation was ensured in the stages of formulation, monitoring, control, and evaluation of social policies. However, more detailed infraconstitutional provisions regarding how society will actually be integrated into this process, beyond mere formalism, were left for further regulation.

Finally, it is essential to consider that new information and communication technologies (NTICs) have brought new perspectives to the concept of public governance, leading to the emergence of a new concept called digital public governance, based on the model known as digital-era governance (DEG). This new form of public governance incorporates digital technologies into the public sphere and governance concept, yet with a more integrative and collaborative view. The challenges lie precisely in breaking away from traditional hierarchical governance logic to integrate society and other actors into the decision-making and discussion structures.

In Brazil, some normative initiatives have sought to bring public governance closer to this paradigm, including the National Digital Governance Strategy, established by Decree No. 8638, of January 15, 2016, which aimed to: I—generate benefits for society through the use of information and communication technology resources in public service delivery; II—stimulate societal participation in the formulation, implementation, monitoring, and evaluation of public policies and services provided digitally; and III—ensure that society obtains information, observing legally established restrictions. With the revocation of this legal document by Decree No. 10,332, of April 28, 2020, a new digital government strategy was established, with a greater focus on digital transformation (E-Digital), defined by Decree No. 9319, of March 21, 2018.

Lastly, Law No. 14,129, of March 29, 2021, known as the digital government law, provided more detailed provisions regarding Brazilian digital public governance. Its provisions are no longer subject to changes by Decrees and must be adhered to by public managers, containing various incentives for citizen participation and social control.

However, legislative innovations, especially the digital government law, do not automatically change reality. Many obstacles and resistances need to be overcome, and pathways such as transparency and access to information, participation channels, data openness, interoperability, and social control mechanisms need to be operationalized to truly achieve digital public governance based on collaboration and participation. Without these elements, only the traditional hierarchical model is transposed to the digital realm.

2.2 What is meant by interoperability in the public sector?

According to Vernadat [11], interoperability can be defined as the "ability of interaction between two or more entities. These entities are defined as communication components between parties and can be represented by software modules, processes, systems, business units, and others."

It should be noted that the concept of interoperability should not be confused with that of open data or data openness. Although they may be related attributes and, in the public sector, are generally promoted, they refer to distinct characteristics. According to Tavares and Bitencourt [12], while interoperability allows for interaction of data across systems from different agencies, entities, or levels of government, openness allows for the availability of public data to be used and processed by both internal and external users. Thus, openness does not necessarily imply interoperability, although it is possible to store these data in another database later to enable interoperability. However, ideal interoperability results from direct interaction with the original data source, to avoid the replication of data and unnecessary creation of new databases by users.

As Almeida [13] details, interoperability encompasses four different dimensions:

Technical/Technological: According to the European Commission (2004), this involves issues related to the connection of IT systems and services. From the perspective of the Administrative Modernization Agency (2013), systems and devices must be able to exchange data reliably and without additional costs. For this to occur, the European Commission (2017b) believes that interoperability aspects should include interface specifications, interconnection services, data integration services, data exchange presentation, and secure communication protocols.

Semantic: Defined as a guarantee that the precise meaning of exchanged information is understandable (European Commission, 2004), including the Administrative Modernization Agency (2013), it is a level of informational architecture transversal to Public Administration, and according to the European Commission (2017b), it ensures that exchanged data and information are preserved and understood throughout exchanges between parties.

Organizational: Based on defining business objectives, business process modeling (European Commission, 2004), so that Public Administrations align their business processes, responsibilities, and expectations to achieve commonly accepted and mutually beneficial goals, and according to the European Commission (2017b), exchange relevant information and meet user community requirements by providing easily identifiable, accessible, and user-focused services.

Legal: Defined as an aggregation point for national and European legislation, playing a relevant role in drafting legislation aimed at promoting and regulating the use of artifacts (Administrative Modernization Agency, 2013). The option to implement new legislation is also advocated by the European Commission (2017b), to ensure that organizations operating under different legal, political, and strategic frameworks can work together.

In Brazil, Oliveira [11] notes that e-Government actions in the 2000s and as early as 2004 created the Electronic Government Interoperability Standard (e-PING) to specify minimum guidelines for interoperability. Currently, this standard is mandatory for federal government agencies and optionally for other government levels and can even be used by private institutions. Interoperability is a complex issue, and when its guidelines are not applied, problems such as data duplication and loss of integrity of digital services arise. Due to the specific characteristics and resource constraints, these problems are even more pronounced in developing countries like Brazil. Therefore, the general objective of this dissertation is to propose a method for applying the e-PING interoperability guidelines in Brazilian e-Government portals.

Within the federal government, interoperability is defined in the document called the interoperability standards architecture, or ePing, established by Ordinance No. 92, on December 24, 2014, by the then Secretariat of Logistics and Information Technology of the Ministry of Planning, Budget, and Management, a Federal Executive branch agency, which sought to establish a "minimum set of premises, policies, and technical specifications regulating the use of information and communication technology (ICT) in the interoperability of e-Government services," according to its Article 1 [14].

Additionally, according to Article 2 of the same Ordinance, the ePing architecture must be observed by agencies and members of the IT Resources Administration System (SISP) "in the planning of procurement, acquisition, and updating of ICT systems and equipment." For other federative entities, including their indirect administration entities, adherence to the ePing standard must be done by their own act, i.e., it is not mandatory.

The Reference Document, in terms of interoperability standards (or ePING), had its latest version in 2018, produced by the Department of Digital Government, of the Secretariat of Information and Communication Technology, linked to the Ministry of Planning, Development, and Management, a Federal Executive branch agency. The document addresses the dimensions of interoperability but only mentions the following: technical, semantic, and organizational. The legal dimension, therefore, was not covered in the document. This is due to the fact that the legal dimension requires the issuance of specific normative acts or approval of legislation that determines interoperability in the public sector, a situation that, until the publication of the digital government law on March 29, 2021, did not exist, at least not in a generalized and applicable manner to all. Thus, there is a noticeable partial update need in the Reference Document, which should include the legal dimension in its next version.

In Brazil, Law No. 14,129, of March 29, 2021, known as the digital government law, introduced, as one of its guidelines, according to Article 3, item XIV, interoperability of systems and promotion of open data. It also stipulated, in Article 20, §2, that the functionalities of digital government platforms should "observe interoperability standards and the need for data integration as ways to simplify and increase efficiency in processes and user service" [15].

Moreover, the digital government law, regarding digital public service delivery, sought to enshrine, in its Article 24, item IV, a principle known as only-once, which aims to avoid, through interoperability, the repetition of "unnecessary demands on the user regarding the presentation of information and essential supporting documents" [15].

Articles 38 to 41 of this same legal instrument aim to further detail data interoperability between public agencies. Article 38 highlights the need for digital tools to consider: information and data interoperability under the management of agencies and entities, respecting legal restrictions, information and communication security requirements, technological limitations, and the cost-benefit relationship of interoperability; optimization of data access costs and, whenever possible, reuse of infrastructure resources for data access by multiple agencies and entities; and protection of personal data, in compliance with current legislation, especially Law No. 13,709 of August 14, 2018, known as the General Data Protection Law [15].

Article 39 presents the purposes of the interoperability mechanism, which are: improving public policy management; increasing the reliability of citizen registration in public administration by maintaining data integrity and security in database management, making them properly qualified and consistent; enabling the creation of unified citizen identification means for public service provision; facilitating data interoperability between government agencies; and processing information from databases based on the citizen's CPF number, considering Article 11 of Law 13,444 of May 11, 2017, which deals with National Civil Identification (ICN).

Also relevant to consider about interoperability in the federal government context is Decree No. 10,046, of October 9, 2019, which "deals with governance in data sharing within the scope of federal public administration and establishes the Citizen Base Registry and the Central Data Governance Committee." The Decree addresses, in Article 4, the levels of data sharing between agencies and entities, which are three levels based on confidentiality: a) broad sharing: data not subject to any access restriction, whose disclosure must be public and guaranteed to any interested party; b) restricted sharing: data protected by confidentiality, but access can be granted to all agencies and entities for public policy execution; c) specific sharing: data protected by confidentiality, where access can only be granted to specific agencies and entities, under the conditions and for the purposes specified by law [16].

Interoperability, in the context of public policy management, is fundamental at all stages, as it allows different public agencies and entities to share data and information across their spheres and sectors of operation, contributing from planning to evaluation of government activity, avoiding data collection repetition, or even producing better insights from data exchanges or application of artificial intelligence and/or data science technologies.

In practice, one way to enable this shared access to information and data is through application programming interfaces (APIs). APIs, in the technological landscape, are an increasingly prominent tool, as they allow integration and sharing of information between different systems, whether from different origins or not, so that they interact and result in specific products according to the need or desired objective. For example, regarding access to public information, the use of APIs allows users to obtain data from a specific public entity without needing to directly access a traditional transparency portal, as required by the access to information law, but they can use programs that connect directly to the machines of this transparency portal and select the desired data for visualization, analysis, or specific sharing.

In the federal government, an API was made available for accessing data from the transparency portal, which is freely available according to the terms established by Decree No. 8777, of May 11, 2016, which regulated the Federal Executive's Open Data Policy. Access to the API is through authentication by the citizen or interested user through the Gov.br account, with a key sent to the registered email for using the tool.

Currently, consultations via the federal government transparency portal API are available for the following databases: Bolsa Família, Emergency Aid, Continuous Provision Benefit (BPC), Child Labor Eradication Program (Peti), Guarantee Safra, Fishing Insurance, Federal Administration Expulsions Registry (CEAF), National

Registry of Ineligible and Suspended Companies (CEIS), National Registry of Punished Companies (CNEP), Federal Executive Contracts, Federal Executive Agreements, Coronavirus, Public Expenditures, Nonprofit Private Entities Impeded (CEPIM), Parliamentary Amendments, Payment Card Expenses, Functional Properties, Leniency Agreements, Federal Executive Bids, Federal Executive Electronic Invoices, Federal Executive Servers, Service Travel, and Agencies.

The National Treasury also provides an API related to the federal government cost portal, which includes consultations to the following bases: active personnel, depreciation, transfers, inactive personnel, pensioners, and other costs. Unlike the transparency portal API, where authentication is required to access the API key, this one "does not require user identification or payment for service use; just adhere to the usage guidelines to avoid service blocking. The data is delivered in JSON format, and by default, queries return 250 items per page" [17].

Various other APIs are listed in the Government APIs Catalog, managed by the Conecta gov.br service, which aims to "facilitate the availability and consumption of data through APIs, and promote data interoperability between Federal Public Administration Agencies" [18]. However, not all available APIs are free for citizen use. For instance, the API for National Registry of Legal Entities (CNPJ) allows querying for obtaining company registration data. Free use is restricted to federal executive agencies that subscribe to the centralized contract of the digital government secretariat.

It should be noted that the CNPJ database is public and available for download by any interested party on the federal revenue Web site. However, API access provides facilities recognized and encouraged by the federal government, ranging from visualization, analysis, to cross-referencing these data with other databases for various purposes. Nevertheless, for citizens, CNPJ API use is available only through paid consultation via a service provided by the federal public company Serpro - Federal Data Processing Service.

This restriction on CNPJ API use by the federal government is considered to contradict, among other regulations, the explicit provision of Article 4 of Decree No. 10,046/2019, which states that in the case of broad sharing, data is not subject to any access restrictions and should be publicly disclosed to any interested party. Additionally, there is a legal violation concerning interoperability defined by the digital government law, to the evident detriment of public policy evaluation, as it hampers potential data cross-referencing with databases such as those related to public resources receipt via agreements, public service delegations, bids, and administrative contracts. This relationship between policy evaluation and interoperability will be further explored in the next section.

3. Evaluation of public policies and interoperability

The evaluation of public policies is an emerging field both in scientific literature and legislation, particularly in Brazil. Decree No. 5378, dated February 23, 2005, which established the National Program for Public Management and De-bureaucratization—Gespública, provided in its Article 2, Section II, that one of the program's objectives was to promote governance in order to increase the capacity for formulating, implementing, and evaluating public policies [9].

The Gespública program was expressly revoked by Decree No. 9094, dated July 17, 2017, which did not address public policy evaluation but rather focused solely on public services, specifically user satisfaction surveys through ombudsman channels. Only later, with Decree No. 9203, dated November 22, 2017, still in effect, which established the Governance Policy for the Federal Public Administration, autarchic, and foundational, did Article 4 set out, as one of the public governance guidelines, in Section III, the monitoring of performance and evaluation of the conception, implementation, and results of policies and priority actions; and in Section VII, the evaluation of proposals for creating, expanding, or improving public policies [10].

More recently, the evaluation of public policies received constitutional status with the promulgation of Constitutional Amendment No. 109, 2021, which introduced §16 to Article 37 of the Brazilian Constitution, stipulating that "the organs and entities of public administration, individually or collectively, must evaluate public policies, including disclosing the object to be evaluated and the results achieved, according to the law" [19]. It is understood that this provision has limited effectiveness, as it depends on the approval of the law, which is still under discussion in the National Congress.

3.1 Evaluation of public policies: From paradigms to methodological approaches

Before addressing the purpose of evaluation within the framework of the public policy cycle, there is an important element to mention regarding evaluation: it is not merely a matter of determining whether the objectives of a public policy have been achieved. Evaluation should also be considered within the context of the decision-making process. The criteria that will be the focus of the evaluation will depend on the areas that the evaluation will address. In an evaluative process, the determining factor is the theoretical conception underlying the methods and techniques of social research; thus, it is not merely a descriptive process but also prescriptive. It is important to understand public policy evaluation itself as a social research activity, and therefore, it is imbued with elements that persist in every debate about defining evaluation criteria, particularly regarding the qualitative aspect beyond the quantitative one. It is evident that every evaluation process needs to be connected with public policy planning, and this, in turn, must be linked to constitutionally established objectives.

The first initiatives in evaluation were observed in the United States, aiming to seek legitimacy in the 1960s, and were later used in European countries and Brazil starting in the 1980s. However, the literature does not show a consensus on a single theory of public policy evaluation. The elements that compose each proposed theory, according to different authors, vary in terms of considered variables and/or perspectives, and they change over time [20].

In this context, a detailed and comparative analysis of these different proposed theories might not offer significant contributions to this work. Thus, a broader analysis was preferred, in which theories are implicitly found within paradigms, views, or conceptions, initially divided into two major categories, which will facilitate the understanding of the methodological approaches studied later.

In line with the historical development of different theories, these initial conceptions or paradigms of evaluation emerged in the post-war period (1950s), in a context of interventionist state policies aligned with Keynesian economics. However, from the 1980s onwards, due to increased scarcity of public resources and a shift toward a more restrained state with greater concern for citizen participation in public decisions, a series of discussions arose to question and reflect on alternative evaluation possibilities from different perspectives than those previously established [21].

Ferrão [21] thus synthesizes two main paradigms: the technical-rationalist paradigm (emerged in the 1950s/60s) and the dialogical paradigm (emerging in the 1980s/90s), with the main elements of each being summarized as follows:

Technical-Rationalist Paradigm: Evaluation is based on neutral (value-free) knowledge, in the form of positivist philosophy. It relies on analytical objectivity through objective and quantitative measurement, as well as evaluator impartiality, rejecting any value judgments. Its assumptions include a radical opposition between facts and values, exclusive use of rigorous, reliable, and valid empirical information, employing methodologies from the physical and natural sciences, i.e., causal relationships between intervention and effects and generalization of results, and finally, the absence of political influence or pressures. Its purpose is to make rational decisions on optimal solutions in terms of effectiveness (results) and efficiency (relationship between means and results). This paradigm prevails in the formulation and launch of new policies, programs, and plans, as well as in evaluating the effectiveness of policies and programs.

Dialogical Paradigm: Based on post-positivism or social constructivism, evaluation is based on socially constructed knowledge and processes of dialog and interest negotiation (communicative rationality). It values human experience, with evaluation having a nature of value judgment or normative judgment, implying that any evaluation is inherently normative and political. Its assumptions include the impossibility of separating facts and values, the impossibility of fully separating science and politics, the competition of interests, which makes evaluations incorporate an ethical and political choice dimension, and the consideration of unequal power relations among different relevant actors, thereby ensuring a democratization dimension during the evaluative process. Its purpose is to reveal the systems of meaning through which facts are interpreted by different groups, ensuring that the preferences, interests, and priorities of all groups are heard, considering that dialog and interest negotiation are essential for establishing consensuses and commitments. This paradigm is prevalent in the scrutiny of new and existing policies, programs, and plans.

This framework broadly shows that the evaluative process fundamentally adopts a philosophical choice, i.e., a paradigm, and the nature of the methodological approaches used, understood as the set of applied methods and instruments, as well as the role of the evaluator, are influenced and directed by this choice.

Regarding methodologies for public policy evaluation, Souza [20] identifies three major approaches in the literature: black box, theory-based evaluation or theory of change, and theory-driven evaluation, which will be detailed further:

Black Box: This methodological approach is attributed to Campbell, notably in the work published with Stanley in 1963. It seeks to point out the results but not the how and why, describing causal relationships between inputs and expected outputs of programs through experimental or quasi-experimental designs based on statistical procedures [20]. Based on the discussed paradigms, the Black Box approach is rooted in the technical-rationalist paradigm.

Theory-Based Evaluation or Theory of Change: This theory is mainly associated with Weiss, who developed its propositions from 1972, and more extensively in the 1990s. Its goal is to highlight that programs have explicit or implicit theories about how and why the program works, and thus, evaluation should seek to identify its assumptions and underlying theories through data collection and information, aiming to examine the effect of these theories on the program [20]. This theory shows a greater alignment with the dialogical paradigm.

The theory can be divided into two sub-theories:

Program Theory: Aims to understand how the program's effects are being realized or not, i.e., the cause-and-effect relationship; and provides information on the impacts generated by the program and on the context and intervening factors.

Implementation Theory: Used when seeking feedback from program staff about how the intervention is operating, or to clarify the variables governing the mechanisms.

The theory emphasizes qualitative methods, although it does not ignore other methods. It seeks to provide a logical structure for planning data collection, focusing on the actual effects of the program, aiming to separate what actually results from the program from what results from external events. Weiss asserts that the theory connects with complex programs where randomization would be impossible, and evaluators need another path to attribute causality between the program and outcomes [20].

Theory-Driven Evaluation: Initially attributed to Rossi and later to Chen, this approach seeks a more substantive theory in evaluations to answer how programs work, the nature and cause of social problems, or even the concepts and techniques involved in social interventions [20]. Like the previous theory, it shows a greater alignment with the dialogical paradigm.

Chen *apud* Souza [20] introduced elements of his theory-driven evaluation to program evaluation that were not present in the traditional perspective. He proposed a program theory subdivided into two sub-theories, which include six main domains:

Descriptive or Causative Theory: Specifies how the program works and identifies conditions related to processes and their consequences based on empirical evidence. It represents knowledge about causal relationships between treatment and outcome, understanding the program's effectiveness, and provides information about the program's impacts and context.

Prescriptive or Normative Theory: Provides guidance on objectives or results that should be pursued or examined and how treatment needs to be designed and implemented.

This sub-theory focuses on:

Treatment: Evaluates connections with desired changes and the fact that planned actions are not always implemented.

Implementation Environment: Discusses how implementation can affect program processes and consequences.

Results: Addresses the purposes of the provided services or problem resolution, the intended objectives, and the relationship with stakeholders.

The program theory thus serves as the conceptual framework for theory-driven evaluation, providing a theoretical basis for designing evaluation experiments and assuming a discussion among involved parties regarding their viewpoints on outcomes and program execution [20].

On the other hand, the dichotomy between the technical-rationalist and dialogical paradigms led to the emergence of new paradigms or views in the following years, aiming to overcome the limitations of both previous paradigms through hybrid conceptions, incorporating mixed methodologies (quantitative and qualitative) and participation in the evaluative process. These include multicriteria evaluation methodology, realist evaluation, and policy reflexive analysis [21]:

a. Multicriteria Evaluation Methodology: Aims to consider the complexity in decision-making processes for policies or programs, given the existence of diverse interests, multiple evaluation criteria that may conflict, and the absence of a single best alternative in all evaluated criteria. The central strategy is to break a complex problem with multiple criteria into simpler sub-problems, evaluating alternatives on one criterion at a time, and aggregating the scores obtained for each criterion using an additive model. The final product of this aggregation is a global value score for each alternative, which allows for ranking them according to their overall attractiveness [22].

b. Realist Evaluation: Shares an approach with the technical-rationalist paradigm, related to natural sciences, by understanding that reality exists independently of our knowledge of it and seeks to identify causal relationships and propose generalizations. However, it emphasizes the central role of actors in the formulation of policies, programs, and plans, aligning more with post-positivist social constructivism. It combines quantitative and qualitative methods without preference, considering actors not in isolation but within the structural and institutional context they are embedded in [21].

c. Policy Reflexive Analysis: Also considered a revisionist perspective, it seeks to overcome the conflict between the technical-rationalist and dialogical paradigms through open and plural dialog between advocates of each perspective. This new paradigm divides evaluation into two dimensions: programmatic and political. The programmatic dimension focuses on the effectiveness, efficiency, and resilience of the policies and programs under evaluation, having an essentially instrumental view but considering normative and political value judgments. The political dimension focuses on how policies or programs and their decision-makers are perceived and evaluated from a political standpoint, focusing on the political perception of the success or failure of the evaluated object through media content analysis and other documents, as well as opinion studies on political legitimacy. As a result, the two dimensions of reflection can converge or diverge to varying degrees.

Souza [20] points out:

"This point is important and deserves further development because managerial evaluation, anchored in neoliberal ideology, has adopted an anti-theoretical discourse and embraced a vulgar empiricism and a quantitative approach. It ends up, in one way or another, negating the epistemological contents of evaluation and its implications for public policies. Evaluation as social research, remember, implies theory or theories, and these, in one way or another, require discussions about the conception of knowledge."

According to Amaral [23], one of the main obstacles in evaluating the effects of public policies is the difficulty in obtaining a control group identical to the treatment group to represent the counterfactual, which characterizes the experimental method. As a result, evaluators generally seek to match units between the two groups as closely as possible using quasi-experimental or non-experimental methods.

This difficulty highlights perhaps the main challenge in public policy evaluation: isolating exogenous causes to the evaluated policy that impact the variable of interest (application of the variable law). Mathematical and/or statistical association methods are used to find the correlation between evaluated variables, but this should not be confused with causation. While correlations have their value, they have limitations and can obscure distortions due to spurious relationships, effects of unobserved or omitted variables, reverse causation issues, self-selection problems, outliers, missing data, and non-probabilistic samples [23].

3.2 The role of interoperability in public policy evaluation: Toward interoperable action in digital public governance

In this final topic, the aim is to connect the previous topics to adequately and sufficiently address the problem of this research. The relevance of interoperability lies, in general terms, in maximizing access to data and information through shared access between databases, especially in the Brazilian public sector, where government databases are fed daily by numerous internal and external sources. This allows for a multi-variate access to information sources by public policy evaluators, through the cross-referencing of databases from various public areas, such as public health, public education, social assistance, geographical and statistical data of the population, budgetary and financial systems of various public entities, data from legal entities and economic activities from revenue agencies, pension information from the body that manages workers' general pension, and so on.

In more specific terms, it has been observed that depending on the underlying paradigm and the methodological approach used for public policy evaluation, different methods will be chosen. That said, both in quantitative and qualitative analyses, or in the combination of these, interoperability can contribute to cost and time reduction, as data can be accessed in a widely shared manner, simplifying measurements for the treatment group or control group in experimental or quasi-experimental methods, or in the application of techniques in non-experimental methods.

In the latter case, within the non-experimental method, the use of the propensity score matching technique is highlighted, which is present in the model only with a comparison group:

Propensity score matching is a quantitative technique, initially used in natural sciences, that estimates—through similar characteristics—the probability of an individual receiving a certain treatment so that this individual, using a propensity score, can be paired with another individual who actually received the treatment. In the context of public policy evaluation, the reasoning follows the same logic: calculating the propensity score aims to estimate—using socioeconomic or other variables—how this individual can be compared (as the "pair") to someone who actually received the policy. Thus, the effects of receiving the policy can be estimated by measuring the differences between those who received and those who did not receive the policy. This technique is used when there is no randomly selected control group to be used as a comparison group to the treatment group (receiving the policy). In this case, the control group is constructed from individuals assigned a propensity score, and the information of this group is paired and contrasted with that of the treatment group [23].

However, it is observed that interoperability in public policy evaluation may have limitations. This mainly stems from the current state of data entry in public systems, which is still very much tied to physical and analog models, where some analyses are done exclusively based on physical evidence or static verification resources. However, this limitation tends to significantly decrease as the data entry method transitions to digital, through the advancement of new technologies, i.e., to a more dynamic, automated model integrated with society itself, without relying, for example, on sporadic and periodic evaluations, resulting in what can be synthesized as interoperable action.

For example, the International Student Assessment Program (PISA), currently conducted by the Organization for Economic Co-operation and Development (OECD) every three years, aims to assess, through a universal exam administered in various countries, the knowledge of 15-year-old students in specific areas, such as reading, mathematics, natural sciences, or financial education. In Brazil, the National

Institute for Educational Studies and Research Anísio Teixeira (INEP) coordinates and administers the test, and in 2018, 10,691 students from 638 schools participated [24].

Even though the test has transitioned to being administered via computer, it remains a static and time-limited assessment. It is understood that a more dynamic and timely assessment could be carried out with the same objective, using and analyzing, respecting data anonymization rules when necessary to ensure student privacy under the General Data Protection Law (LGPD), grades entered by teachers in computerized class diaries/school records, which would allow real-time assessment of students' performance across various ages, educational levels, geographic regions, institutional types, and disciplinary content, all in an integrated, anonymized, and automated manner over the course of the school year. This could be compared with students' performance, for example, through the National High School Exam (ENEM) or other forms of higher education entrance exams.

This digital transformation in data entry and sharing for interoperable action is closely tied to the consolidation of the digital public governance model, based on data governance, which aims to "promote interoperability of information, means of public policy analysis, and more simple and agile digital services for citizens, organizations, and businesses" [25].

In this respect, the fundamental role of information systems and the use of indicators in the context of public policy evaluation is highlighted. As Costa (2019, p. 87) writes, these systems have been evolving since 1960, when the use of this technology was based on the planning–programming–budgeting system (PPBS) technique, focusing on the relationship between objectives and results. With the increase in stored information, these information systems began to incorporate greater complexity, with both prescriptive and predictive capabilities, aimed at supporting public policy decision-making. Thus, information systems (IS) evolved into decision support systems (DSS) and, later, in the late 1980s, into spatial decision support systems (SDSS), "systems that derive from DSS with a strong linkage to geographic information systems (GIS)."

SDSS have some mandatory components, such as a database, information analysis tools, and model-building tools, especially those that allow scenario creation, and a WebSig viewer that integrates the previous components [26]. Additionally, the system should prioritize systemic analysis of results, meaning it should allow for analysis of "cause-and-effect relationships between variables influencing results, distinguishing information reported at various time points," as well as integrating various types of indicators to "ensure the representativeness of specific, general, and strategic objectives, and the achievement of established goals" [26].

Therefore, the use of indicators in information systems contributes to the public policy evaluation process, as it allows for verifying whether a particular public action meets the set objectives, and helps to "improve interventions by considering their successes and failures, identifying responsibilities, and creating conditions to better foster participation in the planning process" [26]. Given the need to collect information to build indicators, interoperability is crucial as it allows for the feeding of diverse sources that meet the objectives and needs, with all its complexity and dynamics, of the evaluated policy.

4. Conclusions

Brazilian public governance does not adhere to a single, pure conceptual model but incorporates various conceptions and mechanisms to guide public administration in achieving constitutional goals. Interoperability, as one of these mechanisms, plays a crucial role throughout all stages of state operations, enhancing and supporting decision-making processes.

In the public sector, interoperability is increasingly recognized as a key variable within the public governance ecosystem, particularly from the perspective of digital governance. In Brazil, interoperability has been more clearly defined within its legal framework only since the enactment of Law No. 14,129, dated March 29, 2021, known as the digital government law. Implementing this interoperability poses several challenges, such as investing in information and communication technology infrastructure, staff training, and fostering organizational culture.

In the field of public policy evaluation, interoperable action can exponentially expand the application of advanced programming techniques and technologies, such as artificial intelligence, artificial neural networks, and data science. This enables more dynamic, integrated, and timely evaluations, all aimed at assisting public managers in fulfilling constitutional objectives.

Finally, it would be possible to simulate the creation of a control group for the use of experimental methods, with the definition of involved variables, thereby addressing one of the main criticisms of this method in public policy evaluation—the verification of the counterfactual. This challenge is often exacerbated by the national or universal nature of the evaluated public policy. These intelligent technologies can also be combined with other methods, either to enhance their techniques, reduce costs, or shorten the time required for these analyses.

This research is limited by the need for a specific focus and exclusively qualitative analysis and did not seek to address specific technological issues. The limitations provide scope for new research and advancement on the topic in different public governances around the world.

Future research can advance the discussion to identify, based on concrete situations, databases that can be made interoperable in order to test and verify the evaluation of public policies.

Acknowledgements

This chapter is an English translation of a previously published article by the same authors: TAVARES, André Afonso; BITENCOURT, Caroline Müller. Avaliação de políticas públicas e interoperabilidade na perspectiva da governança pública digital. Revista de Direito Econômico e Socioambiental, Curitiba, v. 13, n. 3, p. 687-723, set./dez. 2022. Available from: 10.7213/revdireconsoc.v13i3.30240 [27].

Author details

André Afonso Tavares* and Caroline Müller Bitencourt
Santa Cruz do Sul University, Santa Cruz do Sul, Brazil

*Address all correspondence to: afonsotavares.andre@gmail.com

References

[1] Covas A. Transição digital e Inteligência Coletiva Territorial. Lisboa: Edições Sílabo; 2021. p. 117

[2] Bresser-Pereira LC. Entrevista sobre Administração Pública e Gestão Pública. GV Pesquisa: Anuário de Pesquisa, 2013-2014. p. 13. Disponível em: https://bibliotecadigital.fgv.br/ojs/index.php/apgvpesquisa/article/download/58197/56668 [Acesso em: 12 March 2022]

[3] Bresser-Pereira LC. Reforma do Estado para a cidadania: a reforma gerencial brasileira na perspectiva internacional. São Paulo: Editora 34; 1998. p. 33

[4] Castro AC d, Castro CO d. Gestão pública contemporânea [livro eletrônico]. Curitiba: InterSaberes; 2014. p. 14

[5] Húngaro LA. Governança, governabilidade e accountability [recurso eletrônico]. Curitiba: Contentus; 2020. p. 11

[6] Tribunal de Contas da UNIÃO—TCU. Referencial básico de governança aplicável a organizações públicas e outros entes jurisdicionados ao TCU. 3th ed. Brasília: TCU; 2020. p. 17

[7] García EDC. Gobernanza, democracia y políticas públicas. In: Albaladejo GP, editor. Teoría y práctica de las políticas públicas. Valência: Tirant lo blanch; 2014. pp. 413-427

[8] Tribunal de Contas da UNIÃO—TCU. Governança Pública: referencial básico de governança aplicável a órgãos e entidades da administração pública e ações indutoras de melhoria. Brasília: TCU; 2014. pp. 15-16

[9] Brasil. Decreto n. 5.378, de 23 de fevereiro de 2005. Disponível em: http://www.planalto.gov.br/ccivil_03/_ato2004-2006/2005/decreto/d5378.htm [Acesso em: 12 March 2022]

[10] Brasil. Decreto n. 9.203, de 22 de novembro de 2017. Disponível em: http://www.planalto.gov.br/ccivil_03/_ato2015-2018/2017/decreto/d9203.htm [Acesso em: 12 March 2022]

[11] Oliveira A. *Mentes Digitais*: A ciência redefinindo a humanidade. Traduzido por Jorge Pereirinha Flores. Lisboa: Instituto Superior Técnico; 2017. p. 44; 7

[12] Tavares AA, Bitencourt CM. A Lei do Governo Digital e os Laboratórios de Inovação: Inteligência Artificial, Ciência de Dados e Big Open Data como ferramentas de apoio à Auditoria Social e Controle Social. In: Motta F, Valle VRL d, editors. *Governo Digital e a busca por inovação na Administração Pública*: a Lei n. 14.129, de 29 de março de 2021. Belo Horizonte: Fórum; 2022. p. 149

[13] Almeida AP, Vieira M. O papel da Interoperabilidade na Administração Pública: Contributos para melhorar a gestão da informação e a satisfação dos cidadãos Dissertação (Mestrado em Administração Pública). Lisboa: Universidade de Lisboa; 2019. pp. 15-16

[14] Brasil. Portaria n. 92, de 24 de dezembro de 2014. Disponível em: https://pesquisa.in.gov.br/imprensa/jsp/visualiza/index.jsp?jornal=1&pagina=50&data=26/12/2014 [Acesso em: 2 April 2022]

[15] Brasil. Lei n. 14.129, de 29 de março de 2021. Disponível em: http://www.planalto.gov.br/

ccivil_03/_ato2019-2022/2021/lei/l14129.htm [Acesso em: 12 March 2022]

[16] Brasil. Decreto n. 10.046, de 09 de outubro de 2019. Disponível em: http://www.planalto.gov.br/ccivil_03/_ato2019-2022/2019/decreto/D10046.htm> [Acesso em: 2 April 2022]

[17] Brasil. Custos—API de Dados Abertos do Tesouro Nacional. Disponível em: https://www.tesourotransparente.gov.br/consultas/custos-api-de-dados-abertos [Acesso em: 2 April 2022]

[18] Brasil. Gerenciador de APIs do Conecta. Disponível em: https://gerenciador-conecta.readthedocs.io/introducao.html#o-que-voce-tem-interesse-no-conecta [Acesso em: 2 April 2022]

[19] Brasil. Constituição da República Federativa do Brasil. Disponível em: http://www.planalto.gov.br/ccivil_03/constituicao/constituicao.htm [Acesso em: 12 March 2022]

[20] Souza LM d. Aspectos teóricos da avaliação de políticas públicas. Curitiba: CRV; 2019

[21] Ferrão J. Dos paradigmas, práticas e teorias de avaliação às metodologias: uma visão panorâmica. In: Ferrão J, Paixão JMP, editors. Metodologias de avaliação de políticas públicas. Lisboa: Universidade de Lisboa; 2018

[22] Lourenço JC. Metodologia multicritério de avaliação. In: Ferrão J, Paixão JMP, editors. Metodologias de avaliação de políticas públicas. Lisboa: Universidade de Lisboa; 2018. p. 143

[23] Amaral EF d L, Gonçalves GQ, Faustino SHR. Aplicações de técnicas avançadas de avaliação de políticas públicas. 1st ed. Belo Horizonte: Fino Traço; 2014

[24] Brasil. Instituto Nacional de Estudos e Pesquisas Educacionais Anísio Teixeira - Inep. Relatório Brasil no Pisa 2018 (relatório nacional). Disponível em: https://www.gov.br/inep/pt-br/areas-de-atuacao/avaliacao-e-exames-educacionais/pisa/resultados> [Acesso em: 20 March 2022]

[25] Brasil. Governança de Dados: o que é? . Disponível em: https://www.gov.br/governodigital/pt-br/governanca-de-dados [Acesso em: 2 April 2022]

[26] Costa EM, da. Sistemas de Informação e Indicadores. In: Ferrão J, Paixão JMP, editors. Metodologias de avaliação de políticas públicas. Lisboa: Universidade de Lisboa; 2018

[27] Tavares AA, Bitencourt CM. Avaliação de políticas públicas e interoperabilidade na perspectiva da governança pública digital. Revista de Direito Econômico e Socioambiental, Curitiba. 2022;**13**(3):687-723

Chapter 3

Public Policy in Digital Economy Management

Do Huu Hai

Abstract

The rapid expansion of the global digital economy has brought about profound changes to our socioeconomic landscape. Consumers are increasingly presented with a plethora of free digital goods and services, facilitated by advancements in technology such as artificial intelligence (AI) and Big Data (BD), which offer enhanced product recommendations and streamline connections between suppliers and buyers. In financial markets, these new technologies contribute to improved prediction accuracy and the elimination of information inaccuracies. However, they also raise significant concerns regarding privacy and data security. This chapter is structured into main sections: delves into positive impacts of the digital economy; examines the underlying challenges that accompany these advancements; underscores the imperative for governments to actively engage in the digital economy; proposes specific areas where governmental focus should be directed. Finally, concluding remarks are offered in the last section.

Keywords: digital economy, public policy, artificial intelligence, E-government, digital innovation

1. Introduction

The aggregation of assets through digital platforms has the potential to confer immense market power, particularly to platforms boasting extensive user bases, thereby creating opportunities for exploitative and discriminatory practices. These market failures underscore the necessity for governmental intervention aimed at safeguarding the interests of all stakeholders, curbing the misuse of market power, and establishing effective institutional and legal frameworks.

In this era of burgeoning digital advancement, we are presented with a future brimming with possibilities. Each year unveils new technologies and services, ranging from robotics to autonomous vehicles to 3-D printing, alongside the burgeoning gig economy. Within this innovative milieu, the author collaborates with global partners to ensure that nations worldwide can harness these digital technologies to bolster productivity, foster economic inclusivity, and drive innovation forward with research methods as:

Utilizing a quantitative methodology that incorporates statistical analysis, synthesis, interpretation, comparison, and inductive reasoning, the study explores and assesses the impact of public policy on digital economy management. In doing so, the present research used data from different reputable institutions, such as the Statista (https://www.statista.com/). Statista is a global data and business intelligence platform with an extensive collection of statistics, reports, and insights on over 80,000 topics from 22,500 sources in 170 industries. Established in Germany in 2007, Statista operates in 13 locations worldwide and employs around 1100 professionals. The data was classified into different digital economy factors, such as National Security and Personal Data Privacy, Labor Market, and Promote Innovation to consider for this study to analyze their influence on digital economy of the E-government Digital Frontiers—Transforming Public Administration Through Technology. To carry out the analysis, MATLAB software (version 2022) was employed, leveraging its capabilities to process the data and articulate the findings, which are meticulously presented in Sections 2, 3, 4, and 5 of this research. This robust methodological approach ensures a thorough examination of the intricate interplay between digital economy and economic dynamics in the regions.

The factors undergo careful calibration to accurately represent the current digital economy landscape, and the author has calculated and made accurate forecasts with those outlined including externalities and information gaps. Statistical data is amalgamated to adapt of large platforms, foster innovation, establish efficient legal and institutional frameworks for data asset distribution, and implement effective taxation systems for the digital economy. It is crucial to note that the simulations are not designed to predict unforeseen events, such as black swan occurrences; for instance, the global economic slowdown caused by the unexpected COVID-19 pandemic in 2020 and 2021.

2. Perspectives on welfare arising from the digital economy

The digital economy offers a diverse array of products and services not found in traditional economies. Free goods and services, such as knowledge repositories, Gmail's email service, and Google Maps' digital mapping, constitute valuable components of the modern digital landscape. Yet, these offerings often evade inclusion in national accounts such as GDP, which typically assess only the monetary value of final goods and services [1, 2]. Consequently, the digital economy has engendered a multitude of significant services characterized by near-zero marginal costs that remain unaccounted for in conventional economic metrics. This section elucidates several ways in which the digital economy has contributed to economic advancement.

2.1 Harnessing digital intangible assets to enhance social welfare

Data, alongside the capacity to derive value from it, has emerged as a pivotal production variable in the digital economy. This entails leveraging algorithms or data analytics capabilities to extract value across various contexts. However, accurately quantifying the value of intangible assets beyond their mere existence poses a formidable challenge. Nonetheless, intangible assets are increasingly integral to valuation methodologies, as evidenced by research into mass market appraisals. Although a market metric exists for intangible assets, specifically in terms of their net revenue-generating potential, its ongoing improvement remains uncertain. Moreover, intangible assets transcend conventional notions of intellectual property (IP). In essence, the amalgamation of human capital, intellectual property, and data yields a collective value greater than the sum of its individual parts.

The availability of information distinguishes the digital economy, with data serving as a primary reference variable in investment decision-making within financial markets, thereby mitigating information asymmetry. Technological advancements have enabled firms to gather precise, real-time fundamental indicators, enhancing pricing accuracy and reducing information acquisition costs for investors. Consequently, reduced information asymmetry facilitates more informed investment decisions and fosters market efficiency. The advent of big data analytics has also contributed to diminishing information asymmetry in sectors like peer-to-peer lending, thereby broadening access to financial services, particularly for underserved communities.

The digital economy engenders a new externality wherein individuals' information can benefit others, thereby enhancing social welfare. For instance, during the pandemic, digital location data has been leveraged to predict infection risk, informing public health decisions and mitigating economic burdens associated with containment strategies. Additionally, digital technologies, such as artificial intelligence-driven image recognition, hold promise for enhancing inclusivity across various domains, including healthcare, education, and economic participation. Notably, predictive analytics powered by big data analytics enable governments to assess policy impacts in real time, enhancing policymaking efficiency and optimizing social investment outcomes.

In summary, the productive utilization of data contributes to social welfare by narrowing information gaps, fostering market inclusivity, and informing effective decision-making across the social sector. Responsibly harnessing data holds the potential to foster inclusive economic growth and optimize societal well-being.

2.2 Interconnections between supply and demand in digital economy platforms

The proliferation of significant platforms within the digital economy serves as a barometer of market vitality. Notably, both the United States and China boast numerous prominent platforms, with Google, Amazon, and Facebook dominating in the former, and Tencent, Alibaba, JD.com, and Pinduoduo in the latter. While Amazon bears structural similarities to Alibaba, the distinctions between these two giants remain substantial. However, it is worth noting that eBay and Alibaba initially shared striking similarities, serving as models for major platforms worldwide. eBay, in particular, pioneered the concept of overcoming market inefficiencies by facilitating direct communication between buyers and sellers.

eBay's origins can be traced to the realm of collectibles, where its platform brought together collectors worldwide, previously fragmented by geographic constraints. However, eBay encountered a pivotal obstacle to its growth trajectory: a lack of trust between buyers and sellers. To address this, PayPal emerged as a solution, pioneering the concept of escrow-based payment systems. Similarly, Mercado Pago arose within Mercado Libre in Latin America to tackle analogous challenges. These payment systems, initially conceived as safeguards for transactional trust, have since evolved into integral components of the digital economy.

The underlying digital technologies powering contemporary platforms wield significant influence, particularly in bridging knowledge gaps between buyers and sellers and resolving trust deficits inherent in online transactions. Mechanisms such as two-way review systems, exemplified by platforms like Airbnb, further bolster trust by aligning incentives and enhancing market transparency. The proliferation of rating systems, coupled with robust payment infrastructures, enables companies

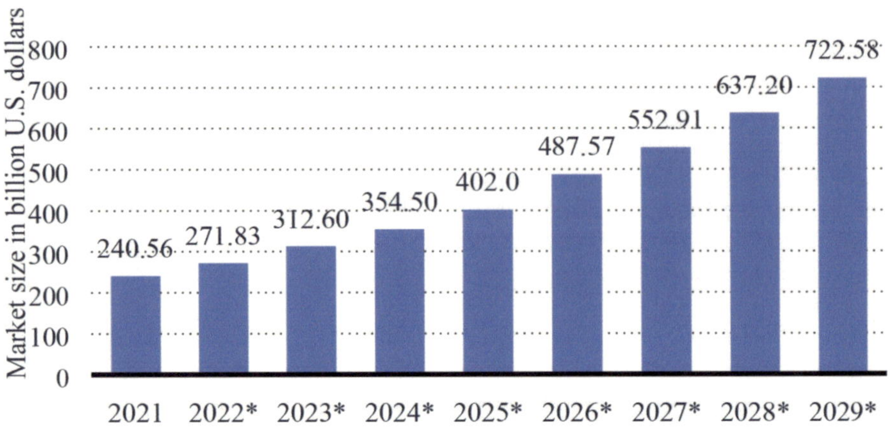

Figure 1.
Size of the big data analytics market worldwide from 2021 to 2029 (in billion U.S. dollars). Source: Author's calculations.

to glean insights and make informed decisions, enhancing market efficiency and consumer confidence.

Figure 1 illustrates the transformative impact of big data on the digital economy and the broader global economy. Over the period from 2021 to 2023, the big data industry's revenue is projected to experience robust growth, reflecting its pivotal role in driving economic expansion. Furthermore, e-commerce activities, crucial conduits linking supply and demand, have witnessed exponential growth, particularly amid the complexities of the COVID-19 pandemic. This surge in e-commerce activity underscores its indispensable role in facilitating economic recovery and catalyzing digital economic development.

The continued proliferation of massive platforms holds the potential to reshape economic paradigms, characterized by their formidable market influence and pivotal role in fostering innovation networks. As these platforms continue to evolve, they stand poised to revolutionize the global economic landscape, underscoring the imperative of comprehensive understanding and strategic engagement with these transformative forces.

3. Challenges arising from the digital economy

3.1 National security and personal data privacy

While data holds the potential to enhance societal welfare and address inefficiencies in financial markets, concerns regarding privacy violations and data security breaches loom large. Balancing the benefits of data utilization with safeguarding individual privacy rights presents a complex challenge, compounded by potential conflicts between privacy protection and public information dissemination. Effective utilization of data hinges upon its aggregation and responsible sharing. However, the rapid advancement of information technology has significantly augmented firms' capabilities to amass consumer data, raising concerns about personal privacy infringements. Although consumers benefit from data-driven product recommendations, they also bear the brunt of financial costs and negative consequences stemming from privacy breaches.

Big data analytics, reliant on high-velocity data types such as clickstream and GPS data, facilitates precise short-term forecasting but also poses grave risks to consumer privacy and security when mishandled. Instances of businesses engaging in data collection and sharing without consumer consent further exacerbate privacy concerns, particularly surrounding tracking technologies like cookies and GPS trackers. Despite yielding valuable insights into consumer preferences and behaviors, data analytics often operate beyond consumers' awareness, resulting in potential welfare disparities, particularly affecting marginalized and less technologically literate individuals.

Moreover, as the digital economy continues to evolve, policymakers grapple with reconciling national security imperatives with the benefits of cross-border data flows. Striking a balance between fostering information exchange for trade, education, and scientific research while curbing spam, piracy, and fraud poses a formidable challenge. Additionally, the emergence of the Internet of Things (IoT) introduces profound security implications, necessitating robust regulatory frameworks to mitigate vulnerabilities and safeguard national security interests.

3.2 Labor market challenges

The digital economy necessitates structural adaptations to the economy and workforce to cultivate productive employment opportunities amid the burgeoning dominance of digital platforms. However, delineating transition processes, requisite skills, and mechanisms to mitigate employment distribution disparities remains an ongoing endeavor. Concerns regarding automation-induced job displacement, exacerbated by advancements in artificial intelligence and digitally enabled robotics, underscore the need for comprehensive social security systems to support individuals and families during transitions. Questions surrounding the viability of basic income schemes and the redistribution of income in the face of automation-induced labor market shifts further complicate the discourse.

As AI and machine learning technologies increasingly automate manufacturing operations and decision-making processes, traditional occupations face the prospect of obsolescence, potentially exacerbating income inequality and shifting revenue shares toward capital. Addressing these challenges necessitates a multifaceted approach encompassing skill acquisition, workforce retraining, and robust social safety nets to mitigate adverse effects on labor market participants. Moreover, as organizations undergo digital transformations, prioritizing upskilling and reskilling initiatives, alongside diversity, equity, and inclusion efforts, emerges as imperative strategies to foster workforce adaptability and resilience in the face of technological disruptions.

In conclusion, navigating the challenges posed by the digital economy demands a concerted effort to balance innovation and privacy concerns, foster workforce adaptability, and safeguard national security interests in an increasingly interconnected global landscape. Efforts to address these challenges must encompass regulatory interventions, investment in education and skill development, and inclusive policymaking to ensure equitable distribution of benefits and mitigate adverse impacts on vulnerable populations.

4. Government in the digital economy

As we navigate the transition into the digital era, it is imperative to recognize the nuanced distributional dynamics inherent in market-led mechanisms. While market forces often excel at addressing distributional concerns, there are instances where these mechanisms fall short, leading to societal discord, erosion of social cohesion, and challenges in public sector decision-making. Consequently, relying solely on a free-market approach may prove inadequate in addressing the multifaceted challenges of the digital economy. Instead, government intervention becomes imperative in promoting justice, equality, and societal well-being, particularly in times of heightened distributional disparities and socio-political tensions.

In addition to distributional issues, the digital economy presents a myriad of challenges that necessitate government intervention, including externalities and information gaps. While technology has demonstrated efficacy in mitigating the adverse effects of information asymmetry, its effectiveness hinges on access to vast datasets. The digitization of information has substantially reduced barriers to accessing and utilizing information, underscoring the pivotal role of government in ensuring equitable access and utilization of data.

4.1 Balancing social and personal value of private data

The economics of privacy underscore the dual nature of personal data, possessing both private and economic value. While data sharing holds potential to alleviate market frictions and facilitate transactions, it also harbors risks of diminishing individual utility and societal welfare, manifesting in phenomena like price discrimination, digital quality discrepancies, spam, and identity theft. A key challenge for governments lies in navigating the delicate balance between harnessing the economic benefits of data sharing and safeguarding privacy and data security. Collaborative efforts between government and the private sector are essential in addressing these challenges, necessitating politically and socially acceptable regulatory frameworks. The outcomes of data-sharing initiatives yield both positive and negative ramifications, underscoring the imperative of informed policymaking and regulatory oversight.

4.2 Balancing digital innovation and national security

In the realm of technology and national security, governments assert their prerogative to intervene in the free flow of information and technology to safeguard national interests. Striking a delicate balance between fostering digital innovation and preserving national security remains paramount for governments worldwide. While governments must incentivize innovation and prevent unregulated market chaos, they are increasingly tasked with navigating the complex interplay between economic dynamism and national security imperatives. For instance, Chinese officials have adopted a nuanced approach, fostering innovation while implementing regulatory measures to address potential risks. However, evolving geopolitical dynamics and emerging security threats underscore the imperative for governments to continually reassess their approaches to balancing digital innovation and national security.

In conclusion, effective governance in the digital economy necessitates proactive engagement from governments to address distributional disparities, safeguard privacy, foster innovation, and preserve national security interests. Collaborative efforts between government, industry stakeholders, and civil society are essential in navigating the complex challenges and opportunities presented by the digital era.

5. The government's specific role in the digital economy

The role of government in the digital economy varies across different countries and cultures, largely influenced by the level of trust citizens have in their governments. In the United States, where there is generally lower trust in governmental institutions, instances such as the FBI's request for Apple's assistance in unlocking iPhones have sparked public protests. Conversely, in China, where trust in the government is higher, there is a prevailing belief that the government is the most reliable entity to handle certain data batches and manage cloud computing systems. The acceptance of government intervention in data management has created favorable conditions for extensive governmental involvement in China's digital economy. In Vietnam, government intervention has been enshrined in law due to concerns over poor control and intervention in response to increasing IT crimes and other illicit activities.

5.1 Control market access, strengthen monitoring of market power, and promote innovation

Diverse motivations drive large digital platforms, with some emphasizing the fostering of innovation within open ecosystems. Chinese tech giants like Alibaba have articulated their goal of establishing low-barrier-to-entry ecosystems to promote innovation and the emergence of new firms. Consequently, it is erroneous to assume that corporations will inevitably abuse their market power solely due to its magnitude. Indeed, large platforms have the potential to catalyze economic activity and innovation by architecting entire business ecosystems. However, the concentration of market power in dominant platforms poses risks of hindering market access for startups and perpetuating monopolistic practices. Governments play a vital role in regulating market access and ensuring fair competition to prevent exploitative pricing practices and promote innovation.

Figure 2 illustrates the steady increase in various components of the digital economy in the United States from 2005 to 2021, encompassing Infrastructure, Hardware, Software, E-commerce, B2B, B2C, Priced Digital Services, Cloud Computing Services, Telecom Services, Services Internet and data, as well as All other priced digital services, and federal non-defense digital services. Specifically, the data indicates a year-on-year growth rate of 12.5% in 2021 compared to 2020, and a 5.3% increase in 2020 compared to 2019. This trend underscores the progressive expansion of the digital economy. During the most recent period of measurement, the digital economy contributed significantly to the overall U.S. economy, adding 3.7 trillion U.S. dollars to current-dollar gross output. Notably, in 2021, the GDP of the United States stood at 22.99 trillion U.S. dollars [3]. These findings underscore the substantial impact of digital services, valued at 1592.22 billion USD, followed by Infrastructure valued at 1167.12 billion USD. Such insights underscore the pivotal role of the digital economy in driving economic growth, a fact recognized and valued by the government. Given the importance of understanding influencing factors in policymaking, this data serves as a valuable tool for informing policy decisions in the digital economy. Additionally, the data highlights the minimal impact of the economic recession in 2009 and 2010 on the digital economy, further emphasizing its resilience and significance in driving economic activity.

In the digital economy, a phenomenon akin to what has been described is unfolding. There has been a noticeable surge in business activity across various sectors, largely attributable to the opportunities and relatively low barriers to entry facilitated by

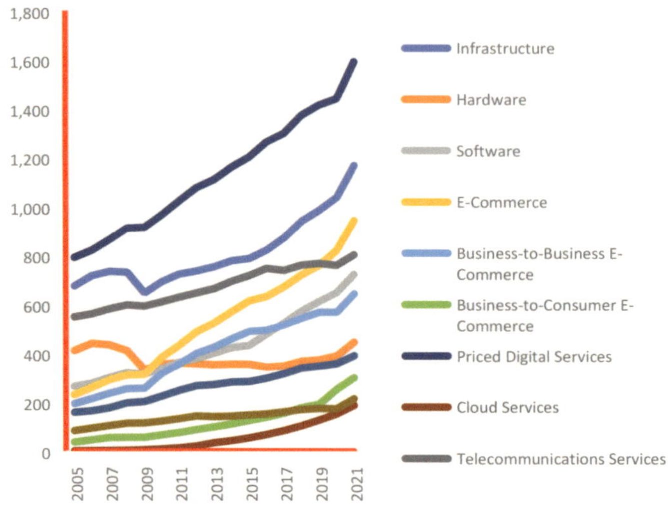

Figure 2.
Gross output of the digital economy in the United States from 2005 to 2021 (in billion U.S. dollars). Source: Statista 2023.

the digital landscape. Central to this phenomenon are digital platforms, which play a pivotal role in shaping market dynamics. However, owing to their data-driven nature, these platforms possess the capability to operate on an expansive scale and scope.

A prime example is Tencent, a prominent Chinese platform commanding significant market dominance. Recently, the Chinese government intervened by levying administrative penalties on Tencent for perceived abuses of its market power, particularly in sectors like online music streaming. China's vast economy hosts numerous large platforms competing across diverse domains, including mobile payment systems. In the realm of innovative financial technology (fintech), companies like JD.com and Pinduoduo, while not reaching the same magnitude as Alibaba, maintain a presence in the market.

This scenario may not necessarily apply to smaller economies; nevertheless, prudent regulatory oversight is warranted. This is because unchecked market access can potentially confer undue market power upon certain entities. Notably, not all platforms exhibit the same level of motivation and responsibility. The concentration of IT resources and digital capital in mega-corporations has engendered novel forms of monopolistic dominance. Exploitation of this power can lead to detrimental outcomes such as predatory pricing and discriminatory practices, stifling innovation in the process.

To safeguard consumer welfare and foster innovation, effective governmental intervention is imperative. By exercising regulatory control, governments can ensure the maintenance of a vibrant marketplace characterized by the presence of multiple significant players. This approach mitigates the risks associated with monopolistic market power, thereby promoting healthy competition and innovation within the digital economy.

5.2 Data in the context of the artificial intelligence (AI) market

The operation of the digital economy generates a vast amount of data, prompting consideration of applying the Coase principle to delineate personal data rights and enable individuals to trade them, thereby potentially circumventing government intervention. Could individuals exchange their data rights to achieve optimal outcomes?

Let us consider DNA as an illustrative case study to address this inquiry. We are nearing the ability to leverage DNA sequencing to ascertain susceptibility to various diseases with a degree of precision. This development poses challenges in the insurance market, as theoretically, individuals with access to this technology would be deemed to have pre-existing conditions. This contrasts with the dilemma of adverse selection, where customers are grouped regardless of their differences, potentially destabilizing the insurance market. In the context of DNA testing and insurance, this phenomenon upends the pooling equilibrium fundamental to the insurance sector. This scenario is not merely hypothetical; historically, I have encountered entrepreneurs who founded an auto insurance company predicated on identifying low-risk drivers, thereby tailoring insurance offerings and pricing to this demographic.

Additionally, we must acknowledge that our DNA sequences possess utility not only for medical practitioners or those seeking to exploit them but also as valuable data for research purposes. Individuals may overlook this aspect when considering the utility of their DNA data, representing a form of knowledge-based positive information. From my perspective, while individuals hold rights concerning their data usage, they do not possess full ownership of their data to the extent that they must remunerate its usage. Envisioning a world where individuals possess absolute ownership of their data, necessitating contractual agreements for every instance of data usage presents considerable challenges that neither professionals nor governments have resolved.

On a related note, the question arises as to whether everyone will benefit from the substantial value creation resulting from the digitalization of the economy. Presently, companies generate vast value from digital and intangible assets with minimal labor inputs, exacerbating the disconnect between job creation and wealth distribution. Consequently, ownership of high-value assets becomes increasingly concentrated, posing significant distributional challenges. While affording individuals ownership of their data appears to address some aspects of this issue, it may not represent the optimal solution (**Figure 3**) [4].

Figure 3.
Market size and revenue comparison for artificial intelligence worldwide from 2018 to 2030 (in billion U.S. dollars). Source(s): IDC; Next Move Strategy Consulting; Statista; Tractica.

Description: Forecasts indicate significant growth in the artificial intelligence (AI) market over the next decade. According to Statista, the AI market is projected to surge from 241.8 billion U.S. dollars in 2023 to nearly 740 billion U.S. dollars in 2030, reflecting a compound annual growth rate of 17.3%. Concurrently, Next Move Strategy Consulting estimates its value to increase ninefold by 2030, from approximately 208 billion U.S. dollars in 2023 [5].

Addressing the conflict between personal privacy and the competitive advantages of data, alongside the "digital privacy paradox" encountered by consumers—expressing privacy concerns yet readily exposing their data—prompt calls for cautious approaches to relinquishing data assets to businesses or consumers. Consequently, the author advocates for government intervention through privacy law proposals, encompassing a definition of "personally identifiable information," the role of consent, and principles of purpose limitation and data minimization. Policymakers are urged to evaluate the merits of data usage against potential privacy risks, consider societal norms, and establish corresponding default standards, all while ensuring the enforceability of data flow restrictions.

5.3 Designing appropriate tax and incentive systems for the digital economy

Thus far, most digital economies or enterprises, particularly in China, have enjoyed tax exemptions. However, in principle, taxation should apply to the digital economy. This naturally leads to the question, "What should be taxed?" Should we tax financial sector transactions, Tobin transactions, or profits, such as value-added tax based on turnover? Taxation within the digital economy poses complexities due to cross-border digital transactions. Traditionally, the tax system's foundation lies in determining where a product is produced and consumed, but in the digital realm, this delineation becomes ambiguous and challenging to trace. Overall, significant tax issues persist in the digital economy, some of which are novel and necessitate resolution.

A fundamental lesson from China's development is the efficacy of government authorities in setting precise incentives for economic growth over the past four decades. As the economy expands, governments garner increased tax revenue and contributions from the private sector in various forms, thereby aligning incentives for both government and businesses [6]. Notably, Chinese officials often prioritize business interests, even extending personal gestures such as visiting businessmen's homes during the Lunar New Year break. Another key takeaway from China's experience is the imperative for governments to remain pragmatic and adaptable to evolving circumstances. Rigidity of thought and ignorance of the dynamic nature of the world must be avoided, with flexibility in thinking proving invaluable.

In the United States, personal income taxes currently constitute the majority of federal government revenue, supplemented by corporate income taxes. Assuming the Internet or digital economy is appropriately taxed and becomes a significant revenue source for both state and federal governments, leaders would have heightened motivation to support the digital economy. The United States is progressing in this direction, with platforms subject to state taxes such as sales tax. For instance, when a consumer makes a purchase on Amazon, the applicable tax on the invoice is determined by the shipping address, varying by state.

This taxation system marks a significant development, considering that initially, online purchases were tax-exempt. Initially, platforms lacked awareness of tax rates across all 50 states, let alone the means to implement them. The right tax policy has the potential to foster greater alignment between government and the private sector, propelling economic growth within the digital sphere.

5.4 Strengthening international cooperation to address new challenges in the digital economy

Intergovernmental and cross-border cooperation in the digital economy is as crucial, if not more so, than international cooperation in traditional trade. Digital commerce offers economies of scale, enabling consumers to benefit from platforms originating in other nations without necessitating the emergence of domestic alternatives. Failure to foster cooperation among governments risks entrenching restrictive trade regimes that disproportionately impact countries lacking successful domestic foundations. While China and the US may weather such barriers relatively lightly, the consequences for Europe and numerous emerging and developing economies could be severe.

Figure 4 illustrates market revenue for AI processors for cloud and data centers from 2019 to 2026, indicating steady growth over the years. For instance, from 2019 to 2023, revenue witnessed substantial increases, underscoring the significant impact of AI processors on the digital economy. Forecasts anticipate continued demand growth for AI processors from 2023 to 2026, highlighting their critical role and the government's recognition of their importance. Given the magnitude of investment decisions, understanding specific products and services' influencing factors is imperative. Notably, the Covid pandemic significantly impacted digital economy growth in 2020 and 2021.

For example, expansion into Europe by US and Chinese e-commerce platforms mutually benefits both parties. Leveraging economies of scale and fostering competition and innovation underscores the benefits of open access within the digital economy. However, reaping these advantages necessitates addressing fundamental questions surrounding privacy, location, security, and data usage. While the optimal solution remains elusive, consensus on countries' sovereignty in dictating their data's usage is imperative. Consequently, data would likely need to be physically stored domestically, controlled primarily by the organization representing the interests of the data's location. Though potentially costly, this structure presents the most viable solution at present.

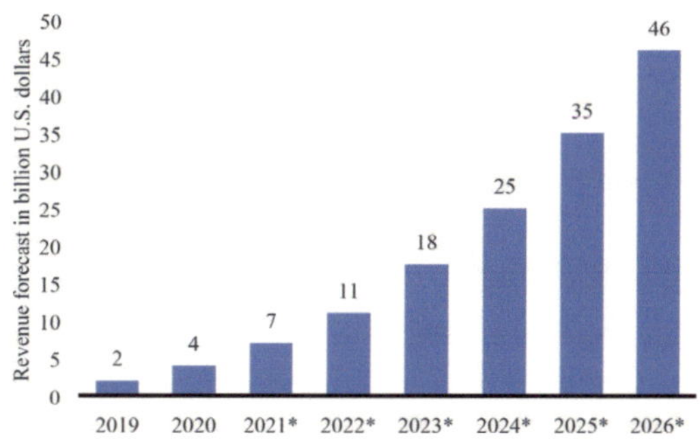

Figure 4.
Market revenue for AI processors for cloud and data centers from 2019 to 2026 (in billion U.S. dollars). Source: Author's calculations.

6. Conclusion

The transformative advancements in the digital economy have brought significant changes to manufacturing processes and everyday life as we approach the digital age. Digital intangible assets, serving as a form of capital, have the potential to greatly enhance a company's production efficiency and market value. In financial markets, the adoption of big data analysis technology reduces information conflicts and enhances prediction accuracy, thereby improving investment efficiency. Moreover, the positive externalities of data in the public sector contribute to generating valuable public knowledge, aiding in public decision-making, and fostering societal welfare. Additionally, large digital platforms leverage integrated user data to enhance the efficiency of connecting supply and demand.

However, the digital economy also presents several challenges. While big data analytics offer benefits, they may come at the expense of compromising user privacy. Furthermore, the unrestricted flow of data, information, and technology poses risks to national security. Additionally, the widespread automation characteristic of the digital economy can lead to human displacement, creating disruptions in the labor market. Moreover, large digital platforms wield significant market power, which they may exploit through predatory and discriminatory pricing practices, thereby diminishing consumer surplus and stifling innovation dynamism.

A laissez-faire approach is inadequate for addressing the complexities of the digital economy. Instead, government intervention is essential to uphold principles of justice, equality, and social cohesion. Beyond addressing distributional issues, governments must also tackle other market failures, including externalities and information gaps, which the market alone cannot resolve. It is imperative for governments to monitor the market dominance of large platforms, foster innovation, establish efficient legal and institutional frameworks for data asset distribution, and implement effective taxation systems for the digital economy. Lastly, in the modern digital era, governments cannot operate in isolation but must collaborate to tackle the new challenges presented by the digital landscape.

Author details

Do Huu Hai
Viet Hung Industrial University, Vietnam

*Address all correspondence to: haidh1975@gmail.com

References

[1] Hai DH, Ngoc HS. Statistical Probability and Quantitative Methods in Economics. Hanoi: Labor Publishing House; 2018. 80 p

[2] Hai DH. Corporate Culture—Peak of Knowledge. Hanoi: Transportation Publishing House; 2016. 55 p

[3] Clement J. Gross Output of the Digital Economy in the United States from 2005 to 2021 [Internet]. 2023. Available from: https://www.statista.com/statistics/962053/digital-economy-gross-output-usa/ [Accessed: October 15, 2023]

[4] Jones CI, Tonetti C. Nonrivalry and the economics of data. NBER Working Paper. No. 26260. 2020

[5] Thormundsson B. Artificial Intelligence (AI) Market Size/Revenue Comparisons 2020-2030 [Internet]. 2023. Available from: https://www.statista.com/statistics/941835/artificial-intelligence-market-size-revenue-comparisons/ [Accessed: October 15, 2023]

[6] Spence M. Government and economics in the digital economy. Journal of Government and Economics. 2021;**3**:5. DOI: 10.1016/j.jge.2021.100020

Chapter 4

Understanding the Essence of Digital Government Diffusion: A Systematic Literature Review

Lingyun Lan and Ellen Wayenberg

Abstract

Digital government has been diffusing across jurisdictions because of its unique advantages in enhancing administration efficiency, improving transparency, and providing better public service. Despite growing research, the distinction between adoption and diffusion remains unclear, and the influencing factors of digital government diffusion are dispersed. To address the gap, we conduct a comprehensive systematic literature review by analyzing 58 peer-reviewed articles from the Web of Science. As follows, we point out that digital government diffusion should be viewed as the process of communicating ICTs through different channels among governments, not being simplified as a single decision step of technology adoption. The four key attributes identified in the definition reveal the essence of digital government diffusion innovation including social system, time, and communication. Following this, we synthesize how factors affect it. The results suggest that the innovation of technology affects users' attitude toward using it; the social system is crucial in determining and supporting further diffusion; the time length allows early adoption to develop into late large extent diffusion; the communication channels shape the way of diffusion. The findings offer recommendations to enhance government capabilities and advance transformation through digital government diffusion, while also providing a clearer direction for future research.

Keywords: digital government, policy diffusion, public sector innovation, government capability, systematic literature review

1. Introduction

Digital government refers to the employment of information communication technologies for improving government administration, which has been diffusing across governments via different paths for different purposes [1, 2]. Digital government has unique advantages for enhancing administrative efficiency and delivering better services to the public. Hence, it is considered an important tool for building government capability and promoting government transformation [3]. Enhancing government capability is particularly important under the context of society transition and government transformation [3]. In the past decade, digital government development has involved more complex influencing factors and challenges. These have impacted the progress of diffusion and resulted in less satisfactory outcomes in enhancing public sector innovation. Some governments have failed to implement digital government due to the limited budgets for potential upgrades. Diffusion in some municipalities is still at an early adoption stage, which restrains the objectiveness of promoting public sector innovation through digital government diffusion [4]. The usage of technology initiatives facially meets the leaders' expectations but does not align with the actual requirements [5]. Consequently, some governments have yet to embed the underlying systems in their government operations and fail to reap the promised benefits of digital government providing more effective services and information to the public [3]. Digital government diffusion still confronts enormous obstacles.

Despite the growing body of research on digital government diffusion, some problems remain unresolved. One problem is that the concepts of adoption and diffusion have been employed together without classification, which blurs the distinction between these two concepts. Studies often fail to clarify whether they are addressing diffusion or adoption, or even regard these as distinct processes [6]. The relationship between diffusion and adoption and the interdependencies between them were often ignored. Karch suggests that diffusion and adoption are two different concepts as diffusion concerns the movement of a policy across jurisdictional boundaries [7], while adoption is the decision to establish a policy in an individual jurisdiction [8]. Diffusion is a part of the larger process of adoption. The interchangeable usage of diffusion and adoption prevents scholars from clearly understanding the logic and process of adoption and diffusion. This results in the imprecise exploration of the causes, characteristics, and patterns of diffusion. Another problem is that digital government diffusion involves more complex forces. The usage and diffusion of digital government are not only driven by the purported benefits of the technology but also affected by citizens and organizational and institutional arrangements. Examining the impact of various forces on digital government diffusion is essential for identifying key elements and understanding how they drive the process of diffusion. Therefore, this systematic review focuses on answering the questions of what is the definition of digital government diffusion and how digital government diffusion has been influenced by different factors. By adopting a rigorous systematic review method, this study reviews the publications on digital government diffusion in a comprehensive and detailed way, synthesizing the definition and factors affecting digital government diffusion and offering suggestions for future research. The results contribute to a better understanding of the relations and nuances between adoption and diffusion of digital government and reveal the key drivers behind digital government diffusion. Furthermore, the review results provide suggestions for policy makers to promote digital government diffusion to enhancing government capability and promote government transformation.

The structure of the article is organized as follows: Firstly, the method is explained; then, the synthesis results are presented; following that, the future research suggestion is addressed, and finally, the main conclusions are resumed.

2. Methodology

Considering the nature, aim, and objectives of this review research, the review method proposed by Kitchenham is the desirable method adopted for this literature review, which is designed to target the soft engineering area [9]. It provides clear and rigorous guidance to ensure the comprehensiveness and rigidity of a systematic literature review.

2.1 Data collection

Web of Science is selected as our main search source, as this electronic database includes the majority of articles in the field of digital government diffusion with high authority. To guarantee comprehensiveness and accuracy, "diffusion" and "adoption" are used as the search terms targeted at collecting publications related to diffusion. As illustrated in **Figure 1**, firstly, the search string "(Topic) diffusion OR adoption And (Topic) digital government OR e-government" is applied to search articles in the

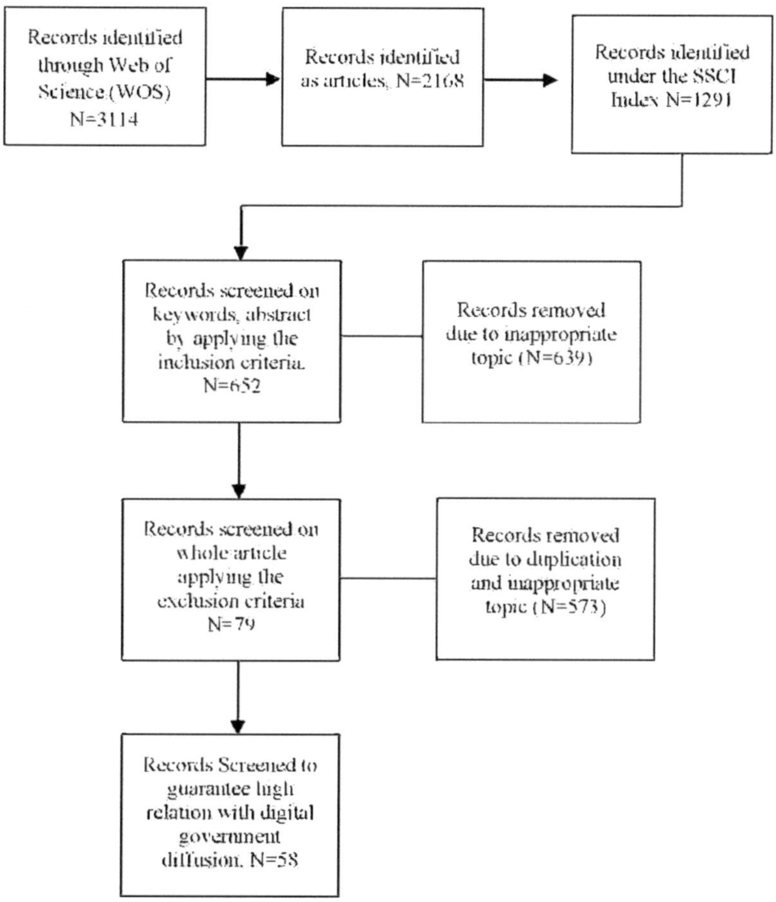

Figure 1.
Process of records collection.

Web of Science, the initial result is 3114 articles. Secondly, applying inclusion criteria to include articles that are peer-reviewed publications; within the domain of digital government diffusion; under the area of public administration or information library science as digital government is also related to information technology; English writing; and were published during 2000–2020. Based on these criteria, 652 articles were initially included. Thirdly, after reading the abstract, introduction, and main part of the article apply exclusion criteria to exclude articles that do not address digital government diffusion as the main focus; articles that only refer to digital government adoption without talking about digital government diffusion; and articles only focus on technology and function of digital government without referring to the diffusion of digital government. After removing irrelevant and duplicate articles, 79 articles remain. Finally, the entire articles were reviewed to remove those with low relevance to diffusion, ensuring that all the remaining articles relate to digital government. Fifty-eight articles that meet all criteria are finally collected. The collected articles involved digital government diffusion among municipalities, states, and countries.

2.2 Data extraction

The development of coding categories aimed to connect research design with research questions and to simplify the coded attributes for validity. Three primary coding categories were established to support the integration and synthesis of our findings: Firstly, a set of attributes aimed at identifying the current definitional state of digital government diffusion by distilling key conceptual dimensions is collected. This includes definitions used, problems in definition, and key elements in defining digital government diffusion. Meanwhile, a set of attributes relating to influencing factors and relevant theoretical lenses used are extracted to answer the second question. Additionally, attributes of methodologies and research dimensions are also gathered to analyze the research landscape in digital government diffusion. The results from these coding categories are synthesized to illustrate the concept and empirical landscape of digital government diffusion research. Then, results from all coding items and the proposed conceptualization are used to formulate future research agendas.

3. Reviewing results

In this section, we present the synthesis results of conceptual analysis and then synthesize how various factors, align with the key attributes identified in the definition, affect digital government diffusion.

3.1 Concept reviewing

In this section, we synthesize the concept of digital government diffusion by showcasing the current definition problems, different definitions employed in the existing articles, and key attributes that should be considered. The results of the concepts captured in the collecting articles show that the definition of digital government diffusion is unclear and fragmented. Especially in defining diffusion, about 50% of the total collected articles do not present a clear definition of digital government diffusion, which impedes the correct and precise understanding of digital government diffusion. Furthermore, the nuances between adoption and diffusion are blurred in defining these two concepts. In 22% of the articles, the term adoption has been used to describe and examine the diffusion of digital government. Some research combines adoption and diffusion as one process, putting more emphasis on exploring what influences the adoption of digital government rather than what influences diffusion. The unclear definition does not explain the essence of adoption and diffusion resulting in the mismatch in the focus of studying digital government diffusion. Although the concepts of adoption and diffusion have connections, they refer to different emphasis in the usage of digital government [10]. Nevertheless, only 15.5% (nine out of 58) articles point out the distinction between diffusion and adoption when referring to digital government expansion usage. The adoption of an innovation refers to the voluntary or coercive process through which first knowledge of an innovation is passed and attitudes toward the innovation are formed, adopt or reject the new idea, and implement the decision [10]. An innovation can be adopted at different degrees, from copying an innovation without making changes to using an innovation as an inspiration. In this word, adoption is a decision step, which emphasizes the first-time adoption of a new idea, practice, or service, by an organization [8, 11]. Diffusion refers to the process where prior adoption of a trait or practice in a population alters the probability of adoption for the remaining non-adopters [12]. Individual innovativeness in diffusion can categorized into five categories based on different adoption sequences, from innovators, over early adopters, early majorities, and late majorities to laggards [11]. This indicates that diffusion is a process whereby potential users are communicated about the availability of new technologies and are persuaded to adopt and use these technologies [13]. Graham et al. suggest that policy adoption studies can be considered a subset of the general policy diffusion literature [14]. Therefore, instead of drawing a distinction between adoption and diffusion, we aim to clarify the nuances between adoption and diffusion, which is crucial for further advancing digital government diffusion.

A clear definition of diffusion is vital. In the existing definition of diffusion, the most frequently employed definition of diffusion is from Rogers' explanation of innovation diffusion, with about 31% of research (18 out of 58). According to Rogers, diffusion is defined as a process by which an innovation is communicated through certain channels over time among the members of a social system [11]. Based on this definition, four key elements are highlighted in the innovation diffusion process, including the innovation, social system, communication channels, and time. Innovation refers to an idea, practice, or object that is perceived as new by an individual or other unit of adoption; a social system refers to a set of interrelated units that are engaged in joint problem-solving solving and it constitutes a boundary within which an innovation diffuses; time describes the dynamic feature in the diffusion process illustrating that innovation decision is a process by which an individual passes from first knowledge of innovation through its adoption or rejection; the communication channels are how messages get from one individual to another, which mainly depending upon a subjective evaluation of an innovation that is conveyed to them from previous adopters [11]. Hence, diffusion is regarded as an interdependent action involving interplays between units. These four key elements also illustrate the nuances between digital government adoption and diffusion. From the time perspective, adoption is a short-term decision, whereas diffusion spans a longer period, involving sequential adoption groups. Adoption primarily focuses on the individual level, examining how personal attitudes influence the use of digital technology. In contrast, diffusion involves the interplay between organizations and jurisdictions, highlighting interdependency as a prominent feature in digital government diffusion. Adoption is a crucial component of the innovation diffusion process and serves as a standard for evaluating the rate of diffusion. However, diffusion cannot be simplified as adoption, as this would oversimplify the key characteristics of digital government diffusion.

To better understand the diffusion of digital government, it is also essential to clarify what digital government entails. The definition of digital government is more agreeable. About 43% of the collected studies (25 articles out of 58) hold a similar opinion to the World Bank's explanation, indicating that digital government, or e-government refers to the use of information technology to improve the business processes and service delivery of government departments and other government entities [15]. The advantages of digital government are highlighted in its definition indicating that digital government usage could advance the competence, effectiveness, intelligibility, and accountability of public government [8, 16]. This supports the notion that digital government is a valuable tool for governmental transformation. The key attributes of digital government include using ICTs to facilitate public service delivery as well as enhancing administration capability. Therefore, digital government can be defined as a government's use of ICTs to deliver public services to businesses and citizens, for improving efficiency, effectiveness, and accountability in public government.

Based on the above analysis, considering the key attributes of both diffusion and digital government, and clarifying the nuances between adoption and diffusion, digital government diffusion can be defined as follows: The innovation of using ICTs to improve government administration is communicated among members in the social system over time through various channels. So, digital government diffusion is a dynamic process where the prior practice of using digital government in a population affects the probability of adoption for the remaining non-adopters. This reveals the crucial characteristic of digital government is interdependence. It highlights the four key attributes including innovation of using ICTs, the social system, channels of communication between different units, and time. Defining digital government diffusion in such a way implies that it is a two-way communication where participants create and share information concerning innovations. Such conception describes communication acts of persuading a client to adopt an innovation in the diffusion process and clarifies the nuances between adoption and diffusion. It reveals that digital government adoption is a result of the diffusion process, where people or organizations may adopt it when the recognized innovation has been diffused. The digital government diffusion process affects adoption decisions, and the widespread adoption of digital government can create a new diffusion process. This definition does not aim to distinguish adoption and diffusion as two distant concepts but highlights the connections and nuances for clearly understanding the key focus in studying digital government diffusion.

From the theoretical perspective, the clear definition contributes to having the precise understanding of digital government diffusion with clarifying the nuances between adoption and diffusion. This addresses the theoretical gap and reduces ambiguity between digital government adoption and diffusion. By identifying the key essence of digital government diffusion, it establishes a crucial theoretical foundation for further research in the field.

3.2 Influencing factors synthesis

Digital government diffusion is not a straightforward process but a more complex procedure comprising a blend of factors. Revealing how these factors affect digital government diffusion is essential to unveil the primary drivers behind and obstacles to the digital government diffusion process. The four key attributes outlined in defining digital government diffusion-innovation, the social system, time, and communication channels- indicate the essence of digital government diffusion. And they also provide key anchors to structure the main factors influencing digital government diffusion. In light of these four crucial attributes, we synthesize how forces from these four dimensions influence digital government diffusion to comprehend the key drivers behind it.

3.2.1 Innovation in digital government diffusion

Firstly, innovation is a key attribute in digital government diffusion. It refers to an idea, practice, or object perceived as new by an individual or other unit of adoption [11]. The perceived newness of the idea for the individual determines their reaction to it. So, newness in innovation encompasses both new knowledge and attitudes toward it. Following this, we specify the innovation attribute by synthesizing two group factors: the technology development and users' perception. 12% of the collected articles (seven out of 58) examine how technology influences digital government diffusion. They found that the degree of internet penetration provides basic support for digital government adoption in municipalities [17, 18], and it requires technical capacity to advance digital government [19, 20]. However, the digital divide significantly hinders digital government diffusion [19], especially in developing regions where it faces many challenges due to lagging technology development. Consequently, this divide poses a substantial barrier to expanding digital government implementation. Even though advanced technology is essential, it is not the primary force driving the extent of diffusion. The more crucial factor is the users' perception of this newness, as it ultimately determines whether users will use it. The synthesis results found that about 21% of articles (12 out of 58) explored the influence of users' perceptions and attitudes on accepting and utilizing innovative technology. Among these articles, five articles adopted the Technology Acceptance Model (TAM) to test users' perceptions. It claims that perceived usefulness, namely the adoption of new technological systems will aid the accomplishment of their work performance; and perceived ease of use, explained as the difficulty in using new technology, could influence one's intention to use innovative technology [21]. Results support that perceived usefulness and perceived ease of use are significant in influencing the intention to adopt e-government services [2, 18, 22]. Another often employed model is the Unified Theory of Acceptance and Use of Technology (UTAUT). It claims four main determinants of the behavioral intention to use new technology including performance expectancy, effort expectancy, social influence, and facilitating conditions [23]. In the collected articles, six out of 58 articles adopted UTAUT and found that attitude and performance expectancy have a significant influence. Respondents with a positive attitude and a perception of digital government systems as useful are more likely to accept and use this innovation [24]. Specifically, trust and perceived relative advantage have significant positive relationships with citizens' intention toward using e-government services [25], while perceived complexity has a negative relationship with the intention to use e-government services [22]. These findings support that as the main users, citizens concern more on what potential benefits they can gain from the use of digital government and the difficulties in using such kind of innovative technology. The degree of adoption among users will promote further new diffusion. To enhance this diffusion, it is crucial to emphasize the advantages and utility of digital government, fostering user acceptance and a positive attitude toward innovation. This underscores the individual motivation behind digital government adoption. Therefore, from the perspective of innovation attributes, digital government diffusion necessitates a robust technological foundation and positive user perception toward this innovation.

3.2.2 Social system in digital government diffusion

Secondly, the social system is another key attribute as diffusion occurs between multiple units. A social system refers to a set of interrelated units engaged in joint problem-solving to achieve a common objective, and it constitutes a boundary within which an innovation diffuses [11]. So, in the social system, it is crucial to consider how the social structure, the norms, and the roles of opinion leaders affect digital government diffusion. A system structure is the patterned arrangements of the units in a system, ensuring stability and regularity to individual behavior in a system [11]. Norms are the established behavior patterns for the members of a social system. Opinion leaders provide information and advice about innovations in the system, and opinion leadership can informally influence others' attitudes or behavior with relative frequency. We examine these components through three factors—institutional, organizational, and political—to understand their impact on digital government diffusion.

As digital government diffusion is an important strategy for government transformation, it entails adapting to the organization structure and institutional regulations rather than merely spreading innovative technology between governments. The synthesis results show that institutional influence attracted much research attention, with 12% (seven out of 58) articles exploring how institution capacity, institution pressure, institution regulations, strategy, and institutional support affect digital government diffusion. It shows that institutional expectations drive public organizations to adopt new technology practices employed by peer organizations [8]. The institutional and administrative capacity could secure the skills and resources to promote the growth of ICT utilization in the public sector [26]. So, a more sophisticated national governance institutional climate positively influences the development and diffusion of digital government [3]. Not only do institutional norms but also organizational factors directly affect digital government diffusion. About five articles found that the organizations' size, status, and budget affect the level of digital government adoption in municipalities [4, 16, 20]. Larger governments are more proactive and strategic in advancing digital government as they have greater financial capability to afford new technologies and respond to external pressures compared to smaller governments. These larger cities benefit from greater administrative, technical, and financial resources, which facilitate the pursuit of alternative managerial innovations [4, 17]. Additionally, cities with a larger, higher level of education, and more politically active population are more likely to adopt and advance digital government than others [4, 20]. Not only the slack resources in organizations enable experimentation with innovations but also the organization's needs may facilitate innovation [27, 28]. Municipalities with more need for one-stop-government services may have a high likelihood of adopting digital government innovation [27]. Therefore, the attributes of an organization constitute the foundational conditions and structure that support digital government diffusion, though they are not easily altered in a short time. Institutional arrangements are crucial forces affecting how digital government is leveraged for promoting government transformation and the degree of digital government diffusion.

Political factors also have a profound influence, with six articles investigating political influence. It confirms that the support of political leadership, political pressure, and political appropriateness are significant in affecting digital government adoption decisions [10, 29, 30]. In the decision to adopt digital government, political support is a crucial factor, compared to the budget and technical capacity, economic considerations, and constituency pressure. This reveals that digital government adoption is an internally driven process. It is primarily influenced by the views of the political leadership [29], rather than motivated by rational economics nor is it constrained by technological capacity and fiscal factors. Political leadership makes a difference and can be both encouraging and concerning. On a positive note, elected officials can promote innovative changes in a bureaucracy in response to environmental changes and public demands [8, 31]. In contrast, political leadership could also impede the process of diffusion innovation for personal political goals. Moreover, the political regime would shape the way and result of digital government diffusion. For example, under the influence of the centralized decision-making system and the "pressure system" of policy implementation, launching digital government projects would become a means of showcasing politicians' ambition and pursuing electoral success [32]. Consequently, digital government is hardly been utilized to improve government performance. Not only within the state, but in the international context political regimes also affect diffusion, the diffusion via international networks is contingent on political regime types [33]. Therefore, political attributes are key forces in determining the adoption and diffusion of digital government. In assessing influence from the social system dimension, it is necessary to consider organizational, institutional, and political influences. The integrated forces from these perspectives could significantly affect digital government diffusion.

3.2.3 Time in digital government diffusion

Thirdly, time is a crucial element describing the dynamic feature in the diffusion process, which illustrates that innovation decision is a process by which an individual passes from first knowledge of an innovation through its adoption or rejection. The innovativeness in diffusion concerns the degree to which an individual or other unit is relatively earlier in adopting new ideas than the other members of a system [11]. So, system members can be categorized into different adopter groups based on the relative time of adoption. These different adopters across time have different motivations. It implies that early adopters seek opportunity framing and are motivated to attain social and economic benefits, whereas later adopter is concerned with threat framing and motivated to avoid social and economic loss [34]. The motivation to achieve gains, rather than merely avoid losses, drives more extensive implementation of digital government [34]. With more adopters joining, it triggers a broader and more substantial diffusion. Additionally, later adopters could benefit from learning the experience of previous adopters to reduce the complexity of innovation and know what organizational changes have to be considered [35], which reduces barriers to advancing digital government diffusion. In the international context, later adopters are also affected by the experiences of earlier adopters. Developing countries concerned with their social and economic contexts may not be ready to adopt the digital government models that are already adopted by the early adopters in the world [34, 35]. This explains why some countries are unwilling to adopt digital government initiatives. The time sequence in adopting innovation also relies on social conditions, it finds that the states that emerge later as innovators are those that have created facilitating institutions and are more affluent and educated states [1]. States that are wealthier and more educated would be more likely to move ahead with digital government [28]. Therefore, different motivations drive earlier and later adopters to adopt digital government. Earlier adoption over time would influence more later adoptions and then trigger further diffusion. Early adopters' success in using digital government would facilitate the motivation of later adopters to join in the usage of innovative technology either to seek gains or avoid loss. Thus, the innovativeness across time affects the degree of digital government diffusion.

3.2.4 Communication channels in digital government diffusion

Fourthly, diffusion is a special type of two-way communication in which new ideas are exchanged [11]. So, the essence of the diffusion process is the information exchange by which individual or units communicates new ideas and practices with each other. The communication channel, as the means to transfer messages from one individual to another, plays a crucial role in connecting two units. Most individuals and units depend mainly upon subjective evaluation of the innovation that is communicated to them from previous adopters. This dependence on the shared experiences of close peers implies that the diffusion process concerns potential adopters' modeling and copying of their peers who have already adopted innovation. So, we synthesize how interaction with peers affects digital government diffusion. Owing to their similar political and socioeconomic backgrounds, neighboring units tend to influence each other to adopt new innovative strategies. In addition, frequent mobility and information exchanges lead to regional comparison and competition that also extend to the adoption of digital government technologies. A total of 11 articles investigated the external network influencing digital government diffusion. The communication channels involve both vertical and horizontal channels, with coercive pressure from vertical; mimetic, competition, and learning pressure from horizontal [36]. All these communication channels play a significant positive influence on digital government attention [37]. In the international context, countries that occupy central positions in global e-government networks are more likely to enhance the quality of their digital government systems [33]. Additionally, global competition motivates countries to invest in digital government to achieve superior e-governance, with leaders influenced by the actions of neighboring countries [38]. Therefore, network connection is an important way that shape the progress of digital government diffusion. It affects how the innovation is being transferred among social members.

In sum, these four attributes constitute the key essence of digital government diffusion. Based on the synthesis results, digital government diffusion is affected by forces from dimensions of innovation, social system, time, and communication channels. Although all these four elements are crucial to digital government diffusion, they play different influencing roles. In evaluating the innovation attributes, technology development is the prerequisite for enabling innovative technology diffusion, but it is not the primary core element. The lag technology would impede digital government diffusion, but more advanced technology cannot ensure further and deeper diffusion. It is more important how users perceive innovation with the ease of use and perceived advantage of technology, which determines whether the innovation technology is accepted. This explains the reasons for accepting technology from the individual level. So, the innovation attribute functioned as the "starting point" for the diffusion process. The common purpose of using digital government to

Perspectives of influencing factors	Sub-categories	Article number	Percentage
Innovation	Technology development	7	12%
	Users' perception	12	21%
Social system	Institutional influence	7	12%
	Organizational influence	8	13%
	Political influence	6	10%
Time		4	6%
Communication channels		9	15%

Table 1.
Influencing factors summarization.

enhance governance capability determines that the social system is the core element in promoting digital government diffusion. Especially, the institution's capability and norms would affect the fitness when the digital government is diffused from one unit to other units. Organizational size, budget, and resources determine governments' capability to adopt and diffuse digital government initiatives. And the political opinion leaders would determine whether the digital government would be used and further diffused to improve the government's administration. Therefore, the institution's norms, organizational structure, and political intention would determine to which extent the advantages of digital government would be utilized. The communication channels would affect the process of how digital government is diffused, and it implies the interdependence feature of diffusion. The time would impact the diffusion degree, but the focus on the time perspective is not much, which presents the weakness in the current study of digital government diffusion. Therefore, digital government diffusion is a complicated process involving integrated forces in the decision-making and dynamic process.

From the practical perspective, the synthesis results contribute to providing recommendations for policymakers to promote digital government diffusion. Highlighting the benefits of digital tools can improve citizens' perceptions to increase acceptance of digital government. Enhancing the support of political leaders is essential, as they directly influence diffusion decisions. Meanwhile, strengthening institutional and administrative capacities is necessary for more effective implementation of technology and leveraging digital government to drive transformation. Additionally, governments should utilize multiple communication channels to exchange information with other governments, promoting diffusion in optimal ways (**Table 1**).

4. Future research agenda

Following the definition clarification and the synthesis of the influencing factors on digital government diffusion, we employ our findings to provide two sets of recommendations for further research. The first set is inspired by our proposed definition of digital government diffusion and synthesis of how digital government diffusion is affected by different forces. The second set is spurred by the results of the field synthesis to propose suggestions for improving future research regarding research methods, and dimensions in digital government diffusion.

Firstly, we leverage our proposed conceptualization of digital government diffusion to propose coherent future research. Our definition of digital government diffusion highlights that although adoption and diffusion have several connections, they have different emphases. Future research should pay more attention to the nuances between the adoption and diffusion of digital government. While adoption centers on acceptance of technology, diffusion involves a dynamic process across multiple organizational units. Recognizing these differences can lead to a deeper understanding of the forces driving digital government diffusion, beyond mere technology adoption. Meanwhile, theories in current research are more focused on explaining individual perceptions of accepting innovation, which cannot further explain the logic and essential features of diffusion. So, more comprehensive theories could be further developed to explain the innovation diffusion phenomenon. The synthesizing results show digital government diffusion involves four key elements including innovation, social system, time, and communication channel. Our results reveal that the attributes of the social system play crucial roles in facilitating or impeding digital government usage to improve government administration. So, future research could further explore how organizational, institutional, and political forces interreacted in affecting digital government diffusion. It could provide insights on how to reduce barriers from the social system to achieve the objectives of utilizing digital government for government transformation. The focus on examining how innovation diffusion over time is rare, and future research could investigate more concerning how is the dynamic process of diffusion. Additionally, with growing research on diffusion, measuring how is the result of diffusion is also crucial, we call for future research to develop multi-dimensional measurements and scales for diffusion.

Secondly, based on the general field synthesis result, we propose suggestions on research methods, and research dimensions for further advancing digital government diffusion research. For research methods, the common trend is adopting quantitative methods, about 55% of research (32 out of 58), to test the relationship between different variables and diffusion. Including employing event history analysis (EHA) on a unique longitudinal data set of municipal digital government adoptions to examine the factors that lead to the timing of the adoption; and conducting ordinary least squares (OLS) regression models to analyze the determinants of digital government usage at different government levels. Although quantitative methods can directly test the relationships between influential factors and digital government diffusion, they are limited to further explaining why those factors affect digital government diffusion. Qualitative research is essential for exploring these underlying reasons. However, such methods are underutilized, with only 20.6% (12 out of 58) of studies employing them. In-depth interviews with stakeholders provide a comprehensive understanding of the motivations behind digital government development and diffusion. Case studies are effective for identifying complex processes and key events over time. Combining case studies and interviews has the advantage of considering the contextual conditions and can reveal the underlying reasons and barriers to digital government diffusion within specific contexts. Future research could employ more qualitative methods exploring how different forces, especially institutional and organizational forces, affect the diffusion process and results, which would contribute to uncovering the deep reasons behind digital government diffusion.

For research dimensions, Digital government diffusion has been studied from different levels, with 41.3% (24 out of 58) targeted at the national level, and 22.4% (13 out of 58) articles targeted at the international level. In contrast, only 22.4% (13 out of 58) articles focus on local government level. This indicates that the research attention is more concentrated on macro levels, investigating the overall situation of digital government diffusion in nations or across nations. However, local governments as the crucial actors in implementing policies whose intention and objectives could affect the decision of adoption and diffusion penitently. Existing research on digital government adoption in local government failed to look at the various types of relationships existing, through ICT, between municipalities and their stakeholders [39]. There is less evidence of the attributes of municipalities associated with technological innovation when it is looked at from a multidimensional perspective. Thus, in the future, more research attention could be allocated to local government's decisions and behavior about digital government diffusion. It can contribute to further understanding the motivation and actual actions conducted by local governments to get insights on how to better improve digital government diffusion.

Finally, this study is limited by selecting articles from only one database, potentially overlooking relevant articles that met the criteria but were not collected. Future research could broaden the data sources by including other databases, thereby expanding the scope of articles and enhancing the validity of the synthesis results.

5. Conclusions

This book chapter presents the results of a systematic literature review of 58 articles based on the method proposed by Kitchenham. After clarifying the nuances between adoption and diffusion, the paper suggested that digital government can be defined as: The innovation that using ICTs to improve government administration is communicated among members of the social system over time through various channels. Following this definition, it has four key attributes: innovation of using ICTs, the social system, channels of communication between different units, and time. The digital government diffusion process affects adoption, and the widespread adoption of digital government can create a new diffusion process. So, the crucial characteristic of digital government diffusion is interdependence. To ensure consistent understanding, the paper follows the four key attributes to synthesize how key forces affect digital government diffusion. The results show that, in the innovation attribute, technology development is not the primary reason for facilitating innovation diffusion but serves more as the basic condition for supporting technology diffusion. Users' attitudes and perceptions toward technology are important in determining whether the technology will be adopted or not, especially the perceived usefulness and perceived relative advantage of the technology. The attribute of the social system plays the core role in digital government diffusion, as digital government is a tool to promote government transformation. In the social system, the organization's size and resources would determine how much support it can provide for digital government diffusion. Institution pressure, regulations, and regimes affect whether the innovation fits into the institution's arrangement. And political leader's opinion would determine whether to adopt and diffuse digital government. The time attribute implies the dynamic feature of diffusion. Time length is the parameter for measuring earlier and later adoption. The adoption over time would provide experiences for late potential adopters therefore attracting further effective diffusion. So, time is a necessary attribute for the dynamic development of diffusion. The different communication channels create ways for information exchange ensuring two-way communications among members, shaping the way of digital government diffusion.

Acknowledgements

This work was supported by the Chinese Scholarship Council.

Conflict of interest

The authors declare no conflict of interest.

Notes/thanks/other declarations

We are grateful for the helpful suggestions from Corneel De Vos.

Author details

Lingyun Lan* and Ellen Wayenberg
Department of Public Governance and Management, Faculty of Economics and Business Administration, Ghent University, Gent, Belgium

*Address all correspondence to: lingyun.lan@ugent.be

References

[1] Tolbert CJ, Mossberger K, McNeal R. Institutions, policy innovation, and e-government in the American states. Public Administration Review. 2008;**68**(3):549-563. DOI: 10.1111/j.1540-6210.2008.00890.x

[2] Mahadeo JD. Towards an understanding of the factors influencing the acceptance and diffusion of e-government services. In: Ninth European Conference on E-Government; 2009. London, England: ACAD Conferences Ltd; 2009. pp. 451-460

[3] Azad B, Faraj S, Goh JM, Feghali T. What shapes global diffusion of e-government: Comparing the influence of National Governance Institutions. Journal of Global Information Management. 2010;**18**(2):85-104. DOI: 10.4018/jgim.2010040104

[4] Moon MJ. The evolution of e-government among municipalities: Rhetoric or reality? Public Administration Review. 2002;**62**(4): 424-433. DOI: 10.1111/0033-3352.00196

[5] Zhang N, Guo XH, Chen GQ, Pacis. Diffusion and evaluation of e-government systems: A field study in China. In: 11th Pacific Asia Conference on Information Systems; 2007; Auckland, New Zealand. Taiwan: National Sun Yat-sen University; 2007

[6] de Vries H, Tummers L, Bekkers V. The diffusion and adoption of public sector innovations: A meta-synthesis of the literature. Perspectives on Public Management and Governance. 2018;**1**(3):159-176. DOI: 10.1093/ppmgov/gvy001

[7] Karch A. Emerging issues and future directions in state policy diffusion research. State Politics & Policy Quarterly. 2007;**7**(1):54-80. DOI: 10.1177/153244000700700104

[8] Jun KN, Weare C. Institutional motivations in the adoption of innovations: The case of e-government. Journal of Public Administration Research and Theory. 2011;**21**(3):495-519. DOI: 10.1093/jopart/muq020

[9] Kitchenham B, Brereton OP, Budgen D, Turner M, Bailey J, Linkman S. Systematic literature reviews in software engineering - A systematic literature review. Information and Software Technology. 2009;**51**(1):7-15. DOI: 10.1016/j.infsof.2008.09.009

[10] Korteland E, Bekkers V. Diffusion of e-government innovations in the Dutch public sector: The case of digital community policing. In: Sixth International Conference on Electronic Government; 2007; Regensburg, Germany. Germany: Springer; 2007

[11] Rogers EM. Diffusion of Innovations. 3rd ed. New York: Free Press of Glencoe; 1983

[12] Khan A, Krishnan S, Arayankalam J. The role of ICT Laws and National Culture in determining ICT diffusion and well-being: A cross-country examination. Information Systems Frontiers. 2022;**24**(2):415-440. DOI: 10.1007/s10796-020-10039-y

[13] Epstein B. Two decades of e-government diffusion among local governments in the United States. Government Information Quarterly. 2022;**39**(2):101665. DOI: 10.1016/j.giq.2021.101665

[14] Graham ER, Shipan CR, Volden C. Review article: The diffusion of policy

diffusion research in political science. British Journal of Political Science. 2013;**43**:673-701. DOI: 10.1017/S0007123412000415

[15] World Bank. New-Economy Sector Study Electronic Government and Governance: Lessons for Argentina. [Internet]. 2002. Available from: https://documents1.worldbank.org/curated/fr/527061468769894044/pdf/266390WP0E1Gov1gentina1Final1Report.pdf [Accessed: 2024-05-06]

[16] Zhao F, Shen KN, Collier A. Effects of national culture on e-government diffusion-a global study of 55 countries. Information & Management. 2014;**51**(8):1005-1016. DOI: 10.1016/j.im.2014.06.004

[17] Sobaci MZ, Eryigit KY. Determinants of e-democracy adoption in Turkish municipalities: An analysis for spatial diffusion effect. Local Government Studies. 2015;**41**(3):445-469. DOI: 10.1080/03003930.2014.995296

[18] Amagoh F. Determinants of e-government diffusion in Nigeria: An examination of theoretical models. Information Development. 2016;**32**(4):1137-1154. DOI: 10.1177/0266666915593330

[19] Zhao F, Naidu S, Singh G, Sewak A, Chand A, Karan M. An empirical study of e-government diffusion in Fiji: A holistic and integrative approach. Public Management Review. 2018;**20**(10):1490-1512

[20] Manoharan A. A study of the determinants of county e-government in the United States. American Review of Public Administration. 2013;**43**(2):159-178. DOI: 10.1177/0275074012437876

[21] Davis FD, Bagozzi RP, Warshaw PR. User acceptance of computer technology: A comparison of two theoretical models. Management Science. 1989;**35**(8):982-1003. Available from: http://www.jstor.org/stable/2632151

[22] Lean OK, Zailani S, Ramayah T, Fernando Y. Factors influencing intention to use e-government services among citizens in Malaysia. International Journal of Information Management. 2009;**29**(6):458-475. DOI: 10.1016/j.ijinfomgt.2009.03.012

[23] Venkatesh V, Morris MG, Davis GB, Davis FD. User acceptance of information technology: Toward a unified view. MIS Quarterly. 2003;**27**(3):425-478. DOI: Doi 10.2307/30036540

[24] Rana NP, Dwivedi YK, Williams MD. A meta-analysis of existing research on citizen adoption of e-government. Information Systems Frontiers. 2015;**17**(3):547-563. DOI: 10.1007/s10796-013-9431-z

[25] Ramirez-Madrid JP, Escobar-Sierra M, Lans-Vargas I, Hincapie JMM. Factors influencing citizens' adoption of e-government: An empirical validation in a developing Latin American country. Public Management Review. 2024;**26**(1):185-218. DOI: 10.1080/14719037.2022.2078500

[26] Kalu KN. Capacity building and IT diffusion - A comparative assessment of e-government environment in Africa. Social Science Computer Review. 2007;**25**(3):358-371. DOI: 10.1177/0894439307296917

[27] Bhatti Y, Olsen AL, Pedersen LH. Administrative professionals and the diffusion of innovations: The case of citizen service centres. Public Administration. 2011;**89**(2):577-594. DOI: 10.1111/j.1467-9299.2010.01882.x

[28] Walker JL. Diffusion of innovations among American states. American

Political Science Review. 1969;**63**(3): 880-899. DOI: Doi 10.2307/1954434

[29] Ho ATK, Ni AY. Explaining the adoption of e-government features - A case study of Iowa County treasurers' offices. American Review of Public Administration. 2004;**34**(2):164-180. DOI: 10.1177/0275074004264355

[30] Glyptis L, Christofi M, Vrontis D, Del Giudice M, Dimitriou S, Michael P. E-government implementation challenges in small countries: The project manager's perspective. Technological Forecasting and Social Change. 2020;**152**. DOI: 10.1016/j.techfore.2019.119880

[31] Mayer-Schönberger V, Lazer D, Mayer-Schönberger V. Ebrary I. Governance and information technology: From electronic government to information government. In: The MIT Press Series. 1st ed. Cambridge: MIT Press; 2007

[32] Tan HB, Zhao XJ, Zhang N. Technology symbolization: Political mechanism of local e-government adoption and implementation. International Review of Administrative Sciences. 2022;**88**(2):511-532. DOI: 10.1177/0020852320915637

[33] Cho B, Rethemeyer RK. Whom do we learn from? The impact of global networks and political regime types on e-government development. International Public Management Journal. 2023;**26**(4):507-527. DOI: 10.1080/10967494.2022.2077868

[34] Ngwenya B, Lubbe S, Klopper R. Institutionalisation, framing, and diffusion: The logic of openness in eGovernment and implementation decisions (a lesson for developing countries). In: Proceedings of the Sixth International Conference on E-Government; 2010; Cape Town, South Africa. England: ACAD Conferences Ltd; 2010. pp. 74-81

[35] Korteland E, Bekkers V. The diffusion of electronic service delivery innovations in Dutch e-policing: The case of digital warning systems. Public Management Review. 2008;**10**(1):71-88. DOI: 10.1080/14719030701763195

[36] Homburg V, Dijkshoorn A, Thaens M. Diffusion of personalised services among Dutch municipalities: Evolving channels of persuasion. Local Government Studies. 2014;**40**(3):429-450. DOI: 10.1080/03003930.2013.795892

[37] Pan TT, Fan B. Institutional pressures, policy attention, and e-government service capability: Evidence from China's prefecture-level cities. Public Performance & Management Review. 2023;**46**(2):445-471. DOI: 10.1080/15309576.2023.2169834

[38] Lee CP, Chang K, Berry FS. Testing the development and diffusion of e-government and e-democracy: A global perspective. Public Administration Review. 2011;**71**(3):444-454. DOI: 10.1111/j.1540-6210.2011.02228.x

[39] Nasi G, Frosini F, Cristofoli D. Online service provision: Are municipalities really innovative? The case of larger municipalities in Italy. Public Administration. 2011;**89**(3):821-839. DOI: 10.1111/j.1467-9299.2010.01865.x

Section 2

Digital Transformation

Chapter 5

Prolegomenon on the Implementation of Artificial Intelligence in Notarial Competencies in Ecuador: A Legal-Critical Approach

Luis Eduardo Rengifo Aispur and Freddy Patricio Torres Briones

Abstract

The Ecuadorian notarial system, with more than 200 years of history, faces challenges in the digital age. The implementation of technologies, such as blockchain and artificial intelligence (AI), could revolutionize notarial practices. Although blockchain offers immutability and security, it would not completely replace the Latin notary, whose functions go beyond mere authentication. AI, through Machine Learning and Deep Learning, could assist in tasks, such as document review, verification of legal requirements and detection of inconsistencies in contracts. A hybrid model with the use of an automated platform with AI, and the functions of the notary, would combine human experience with technological efficiency. This would require an update of the legal framework, investment in infrastructure and training. The digitization of documents and the creation of a decentralized and permissioned platform would improve the accessibility and efficiency of notarial services. The change faces resistance in a traditionally conservative sector. However, following examples such as the *SIGNO* platform in Spain, Ecuador could gradually modernize its notarial system, maintaining the essence of public faith while taking advantage of the benefits of new technologies.

Keywords: Legal Tech, Notary Law, Comparative Law, artificial intelligence, legal certainty

1. Introduction

Artificial intelligence (AI), two words that in contemporary times sound in all areas of human interaction, sometimes out of curiosity, other times with mystery, even with fear of what it encompasses and the potential of this new form of technology that has changed this digital era. This new technological development is here to stay; and, as Oppenheimer says, it is necessary that, at least in the workplace, professionals adapt to these new forms of applied sciences, to make the most of them and benefit from their qualities [1]. Of course, with the adequate security that must be implemented in order not to incur in a violation of Human Rights.

Now, the subject of Human Rights has been touched, so it is necessary to move momentarily to the field of Law, since this essay seeks at least prima facie to *give* certain guidelines on important concepts of AI so that it can be implemented in one of the functions of great importance of legal life, that is, Notarial Law. Therefore, this study seeks to immerse itself in a fascinating and for the moment little-explored territory, such as the implementation of AI in the sphere of the activities of the Notarial Service in Ecuador.

There is a fluctuation between what is advanced technology and its implementation in legal systems, understanding that when referring to legal systems, it does not refer to digital systems, rather, it refers to systems, such as the form, organization, methodology and technique that the legal systems that govern a State have. There are many challenges for the implementation of technology not only in the field of Law, but in several fields and disciplines where AI can be used, however, the opportunities it offers are truly unimaginable.

As this short research progresses, questions will be answered and very important concepts will be discussed, such as: *What is the Notarial service? What is public faith? What do Blockchain concepts encompass? What are Smart Contracts? What is meant by digital identity?*, among others. Although it is a prolegomenon, that is, a pre-seminal study, the main issue of ethics for the use of AI cannot be left aside, especially because when looking for the configuration, and giving certain references for its implementation in notarial service, it touches on issues, such as the certification of documents that must be authentic, verification of identities and competencies that are essential in this state function.

This introductory essay on this casuistry also seeks in some way to stimulate and encourage the dialog, or necessary debate between experts in the field of technological sciences, jurists passionate about the way in which Law should act, in the face of these changes in digital paradigms with the advance of AI, and of course with the union of these specialists. With an adequate dialectical exercise, continue to promote the hermeneutical and epistemic bases, for adequate legal development, which above all adapts to these new trends, with precision and caution of course, considering that the human factor, human dignity, must always be the center of all progress within the different disciplines, including of course the sciences of computer technology.

Well, once the most relevant aspects of all the elements that make up the theme of this short study have been collected, it is necessary to briefly and in a general way reply to both the questions posed and the concepts previously wielded in the preceding lines; for which, it is necessary to start with one of the main variables of this proposal, in this sense.

1.1 What is the notarial service?

This point is of great importance within the introductory development of this research work, since it is one of the crucial elements of the topic raised. The notarial system in most countries makes a solid reference to determining notaries as those officials within the field of public law or public management, whose service and instruction is based on receiving the actions and contracts that the people who have entered them wish to give them a sense of true authenticity. This, of course, together with the documents issued by a public authority and to ensure their date, to preserve them, that is, to keep an adequate record of them, to issue copies and certified documentary expeditions [2].

The standard definition of the notarial service is taken from the famous French Law of Ventose, proclaimed in the year XI, exactly on March 16, 1803, the same conceptualization that was coined by neighboring countries, such as Belgium and Luxembourg. Germany, in the same way, in the Federal Law on Notaries *(Bundesnotarordnung)*, established a definition of notary and what it entails with the notarial service like those of these European countries already mentioned. It is necessary to add something quite curious within the history of this topic, and it is since France and Luxembourg replaced the name of *fonctionaire* with *Officer public*, resulting in a distinction between what is a public official, a public servant and those officials of the State who have a public delegation in their name [2]. This final form of separation of terms and understanding of the figure of the notary has been expanded to most countries in whose legal systems, and this delegation of public power is established to provide public attestation of the certainty of the actions with physical or digital documentary support, as in the case of Ecuador that handles these competencies for Notaries.

Now, with these ideas embodied, it is important to propose some definitions by country, so that there is a clear understanding of what the notarial service entails. In Spain, the definition of notary states: "*The notary is the public official authorized to attest, in accordance with the laws, to contracts and other extrajudicial acts. There shall be in the whole kingdom only one class of these officials*" [2]. This information is extracted from the Law of Notaries of May 28, 1862.

In Italy, the concept given to notaries lies in the fact that "*Notaries are public officials instituted to receive documents between the living or of the last will, to attribute public faith to them, to keep them in deposit, to issue copies, certificates or extracts*" [2]. This information is extracted from the Notarial Ordinance.

In Holland, the office of the notary is spoken of as follows: "The office of the Notary gives the notary the power to draw up authentic documents in the case in which the law obliges or when a party demands them, as well as to perform other tasks imposed on him by law" [2]. This information is taken from the Law on the Office of Notaries of April 16, 1998.

Information has been taken from the old laws that give rise to the conceptualization of the notary and his competencies in the notarial service; to exemplify that from those years to the present, the functions of the Notaries' Offices have not changed to a great extent, maintaining these functions and denominations of the activities of the notary. In Ecuador, Article 6 of the Notarial Law stipulates that: "*Notaries are officials invested with public faith to authorize, at the request of a party, the acts, contracts and documents determined in the Laws*" [3]. This legal regulation has its last reform in 2022, so it is evident that, as already mentioned, the functions of Notaries have not changed since the times of its state and legal formalization.

1.2 What is public faith?

When referring to public faith, it must be taken into consideration initially that it is born from the legitimacy that is granted by the decision of the people and that it is enshrined in the Constitution, since, since the will of the sovereign is translated into the fundamental political charter of a Nation, the competencies, attributions and faculties, given to the *Notarial Function*, are designs of the population, therefore, from there the public faith is born.

Now, specifically to the technical part of what makes up the public faith, it should be noted that this is the essential function that a notary has, to authenticate or give as effective and reliable, those actions or contractual relationships that occur between people and which to have a legitimate effect are carried out before a notary [4]. In this sense, these documents endowed with public faith serve as full proof of being totally authentic documents.

Article 7 of the Notarial Law that governs the Republic of Ecuador states: "*Each Notary shall exercise his function within the canton for which he has been appointed, regardless of the domicile of the grantors, the location of the assets subject to the act or contract or the place of fulfillment of the obligations*" [3]. Although this article refers to the fact that Notaries' Offices are divided into cantons, of course, depending on the need that exists, with emphasis on population demographics. The *public faith radiates* to the entire Ecuadorian territory, so that acts or contracts can be entered into at any notary in the country, no matter if the grantors' domicile is in another city, if it is stated that they are in the place where the notarial certification is to be carried out, therefore, as can be observed, public faith is throughout the national territory.

1.3 Artificial intelligence and law

The development of technology is undoubtedly unstoppable, it has become a central and primordial part of the human being, in all areas. It is often said that the best results and opportunities for the future come out of great crises. COVID undoubtedly brought an unprecedented human crisis, where barbarities, atrocities and fear took over the entire planet. Apart from all these bleak scenarios, in the field of technology, it was a deployment of its use and advancement and implementation in all areas at least of human interconnectivity.

However, there is the other side of the coin, the one pointed out by Byun Chul-Han, Noah Yuval Harari or Shoshana Zuboff, as they warn of the dangers and dystopias that the excessive use of technology and above all the radical advance of it can bring [5]. These authors, whose thoughts are compiled in Rivero Ortega's work, analyze the fact that the dependence that the use of technology has generated is worrying, since they could turn humanity into something very different from what was normally conceived of in ancient times, generating a dead-end hybrid between naturalization and tools.

Every advance entails a risk that is evident, and this has been seen throughout history, that is why in this contemporary space of application of new forms of technology, the role of the law is essential, in order to protect freedom, privacy, prevent and above all put a clear limit to the appropriate use of these advances such as AI [5]. For this, the role of legislators and the correct advice to them are very important, who in their hands have the law-making figure that not only needs the appropriate parliamentary technique, but also the essential knowledge of what technology called AI implies.

1.4 Ethics as an essential tool for artificial intelligence (AI)

Ethics, indispensable in all disciplines and why not say, in all forms of human activity, its use is necessary more than ever, is the key point of the *deontological part* of the good management of the new technological realities. The duty to be *(deontology)*, a fundamental axiom for the way in which digital tools must be used, is essential, as a council of experts that adequately guide the abuses and excesses that artificial intelligence can have [5].

"*Ethics serves to guide appropriate conduct, but it does not allow obligations to be pointed out or sanctions imposed for their compliance. We should not be surprised, then, by the funding received by a growing number of centers and institutes on the ethics of artificial intelligence*" [5]. Rivero Ortega proposes a clear idea about the capitalization that the growing fever of artificial intelligence and its use has had, taking into consideration that beyond all centers, institutes, schools, etc., what is necessary is to promote a culture of clear ethics about how artificial intelligence should be for the proper use and exploitation of it, establishing the risks and problems that could lead to its malfunction and wear and tear for negative objects.

At the present time, within what is the legal doctrine regarding the implementation of artificial intelligence, it is highlighted that there is really a lack of technical criteria regarding the science behind intelligence, to be able to contribute with exact methods or, at least, sufficient, in order to achieve an adequate regulation as close as possible to the idea of what is really needed in the regulation of artificial intelligence.

1.5 The new form of identity? Digital identity?

To concentrate all the necessary components for a correct understanding of what is needed to formulate an adequate prolegomenon of ideas and guidelines on implementing artificial intelligence (AI) in the Notarial function of Ecuador, since, although it is a legal approach, it is necessary to take certain keys as necessary elements in this fusion of information technologies with this public faith service.

Therefore, it is imperative to highlight certain realities in today's times, normally within the interaction of people, for digital tools, at least in social networks, it is necessary to emphasize that information must be provided as a set of data that is presented on the screen and that, in the cases of the creation of a truthful or reliable profile, these are undoubtedly going to belong to a real person.

With this criterion, it is possible to highlight the fact that in the division of the analog with the digital, there is within the figure of the human being, a physical identity, but undoubtedly now, a digital identity that represents that person in the cybernetic world, for which this representation must be controlled by the person to whom it is represented. Of course, in a *normal case*, however, also in those cases where a person uses false information, in one way or another there is information on the network that represents an *avatar* controlled by this person.

Some authors point out that, "*beyond digital identity, we must speak of the accreditation of the person's identity by digital or electronic means, because the person remains an osla, even if he or she interacts in different communities*" [6]. However, these terms' *digital identity* points to the fact that a person, by handing over their information to a digital platform, is somehow forming an identity in the cyberspace that represents them.

1.6 Legal Tech and blockchain

Basically, this digital figure of new information technologies is an expression that has expanded throughout the world, which is why it has been used in several of the new digital operations that exist such as *fintech* or the implementation of technological development and AI in finance. "*Blockchain is a distributed database, that is, decentralized or operated from different points of service or nodes of a network, whose technical foundations are anchored in the so-called Distributed-Leger Technology (DLT), and which is based on these essential configuring notes*" [7]. The central effect or central importance of this type of technology lies in the existence of data divided into unique blocks by chains of electronic signatures with an algorithm of organization and chronological systematization of double keys, this is divided by a first, where it can be operated by the public and the other that is in fact operated privately *asymmetric cryptography*.

Well, an essential component in this system of data chains is undoubtedly the work carried out by the *nodes*, which are basically computers or devices, which essentially base their operation on storing partial or complete copies of the blockchain. They are responsible for verifying and overvalidating the authenticity of new transactions that are made in the data chains. They transmit the essential information they store about preexisting transactions and blocks to other nodes. Finally, they help maintain the total integrity and security of the network to safeguard the information contained in it.

It is necessary to complement this small introductory section of concepts, to refer to what the new *expression LegalTech* means, since in essence this term refers to the area of the *Commonwealth*, as specifically in the origin of the help that small and medium-sized enterprises (SMEs) provide to law firms, providing them with specialization in technology, legal resources, as well as technological tools focused on making the legal profession more efficient and effective [7]. In other words, with the use of the help of digitalization and technological instruments, the work of lawyers can be carried out in less time and investing fewer resources.

LegalTech, as an expression, was originally coined in the United States around the 1990s, as a part of great value and importance of the phenomenon that was recurrent at that time in the reality of public and private finance known as *fintech*. This phenomenon is of great relevance specifically with the development and work activity of the large law firms that exist, which require several different services, such as specialized financial advice with the implementation of digital systems that guide these ways of doing finance [7]. In Europe, in the United Kingdom, fintech and LegalTech services are often used as a specific form of financial and legal advice.

Thus, the implementation of LegalTech is characterized by all these processes of automation of the organization of judicial cases, projects focused on the legal field, very important selection of the legal rules applicable to specific cases and, in addition, on the economic level, the processes that are directly related to the forms of payment, invoicing to customers, management of documentation and digital archiving of the same.

Linked to the central theme of this research, regarding the implementation of artificial intelligence in the legal field, we must in Chinese courts of justice, LegalTech tools, such as AI, are already used to resolve real legal cases. AI-related technological assistants are used to collate evidence, verify information and even predict sentences; they are also essential in the reliability of sources and impartiality in the handling of information [8]. The Chinese government is actively supporting industries and investing in the development of AI, including implementing them in the different branches of the central government to improve their activities, competencies and attributions.

1.7 Smart legal contracts

The theoretical computer scientist Nick Szabo, creator of *Smart Contracts* in 1996, gave a great advance to the legal society with the implementation of the electronic contract. This contract has some special characteristics, in which the clauses that make it up, especially those of the pecuniary issues, obligations and object of the contract, are automated by software and hardware elements [9]. However, this type of contract faces several types of challenges, related to its practical application in some contractual relationships, in which it generates a great problem when it comes to its application.

This problem is involved in the fact that this type of contract often leaves aside the essence determined in what is known as the *legal business*, which is based on the agreement of wills to comply with a certain purpose, take into account that for this it is necessary to comply with certain elements, such as: the capacity of the parties, understood as that form of compliance with the legal requirements, being a person of legal age and duly exercising their fundamental rights, another requirement that makes the legal transaction is that the contract has a lawful object, that is, the obligations of the contracting parties are fixed in matters of legality, what is known as the Latinism *quid pro quo* something in exchange for something is also necessary, thus perfecting the legal business between the parties.

The transition from the *smart contract* to the *smart legal contract* is based on the characteristic that it is sought under all criteria to comply with the voluntary legal business that is agreed between the parties. Now, it is important to note that it was the Canadian jurist Joe Stark who first used the term smart legal contract in 2016. Thus, "*the smart legal contract refers to those electronic legal transactions in which the program that automatically executes all or some of the obligational considerations is inserted in a certain blockchain*" [9].

2. Methodology

This academic study is mainly oriented toward a qualitative methodology, with the purpose of examining the extensive literature that exists on the central theme and relating it to the object of analysis of each element that makes it up.

Due to its scope, the study is largely descriptive, using an empirical-theoretical procedure based, as already mentioned, on a rigorous bibliographic review and collection of information. Likewise, this work adopts an explanatory approach, by analyzing the relationship and components surrounding intelligence for its implementation in the Ecuadorian notarial system.

The research has focused on compiling and analyzing various academic works carried out by leading experts in the field, as well as describing the applicable regulations, to identify the central problem and direct efforts toward obtaining expected results, which are based on forming the prolegomenon with clear ideas on how the implementation of artificial intelligence in the notarial system of Ecuador could be.

Now, it is a qualitative approach, since, due to the subject matter of this study, it was necessary to carry out an exhaustive analysis of the existing literature-doctrine to date, which is known as the state of the art of a research; therefore, a detailed understanding of the elements that make up the implementation of AI in the notarial system is necessary. To move to its application in the Ecuadorian notarial system, it is essential to meet the objectives of the research. Therefore, this type of qualitative approach made it possible to examine in detail and adequately relate the factors that make up the phenomenon in a more holistic way [10].

Finally, the benefit of descriptive and explanatory methodological scope allows for a comprehensive and centralized understanding of the topic addressed [10]. In the same way, it facilitates a broad identification of the central problem to achieve the fulfillment of the objective of this research, formulating concrete proposals regarding the implementation of intelligent augmentation (IA) in the Ecuadorian notarial system. This, as has already been said, using clear factors and components that form this study objective, generating clear ideas as a prolegomenon to fulfill the theme of this research work.

3. Results

3.1 Blockchain and smart legal contracts

Blockchain is a database that has a decentralized systems architecture model, and this type of database operates from several servers or nodes of the network which will manage and process the information that will be part of that database, so it is also important to note that this type of database can even be self-managed to achieve decision-making, this without depending on a centralized entity, that is, each of the collaborators, servers, nodes, etc., operates on an equal footing (peer-to-peer (P2P)).

This type of database has an unrestricted link with digital financial technology (fintech), and both its development and implementation were made at the same time as the creation of cryptocurrencies and especially bitcoin, precisely to provide security and reliability to this digital financial technology, using a cryptography system that allows it to assign a unique identifier to each of the blocks that will be part of the chain. This identifier that is generated for each block is part of the next block linking them and ensuring their immutability, since the slightest variation of one block causes the others to not be authenticated, a situation that allows us to trust the information stored in each block.

In addition, this system has another verification system to be able to correctly link each of the blocks that are added to the chain, and for this it is necessary to analyze two points that were stated above and these are self-management for decision-making and peer-to-peer operation between the different nodes, because it is precisely these elements that are responsible for this other form of verification called proof of work (POW), which basically consists of a series of mathematical problems and algorithmic labyrinths that must be solved in a specific time.

In the case of bitcoin blocks, the proof of work lasts 10 minutes, and if the collaborator, server or node solves them, they receive a reward and thus also help to verify and add the said block to the chain, a situation that complicates the possibility of a hack or violation of one of these blocks, because in order to modify and add that block to the chain, a vast amount of resources would be needed to the processing[1] of that information and equaling the longest chain, a situation that is another determining factor in blockchains since the most extensive blockchain is the one that survives.

With this limitation that exists to modify a block of the chain and its subsequent validation or verification, this system guarantees the invulnerability and security with respect to the information contained in each block, in addition to becoming a kind of public records of previous actions, as well as with regard to bitcoins. These blocks or records allow us to make visible each of the transactions made, thus not being able to depend on a centralized system to corroborate the existence of funds of a certain individual, since it would be enough to review the previous records that appear in the chain.

As we can see, the system proposed by blockchains seeks to guarantee and support the information that appears in each of its records, and although it has found its development with digital financial technology, it is not exempt from being able

[1] When any modification occurs to a block in the chain, this block will automatically be assigned a new identification number, which must necessarily be linked to a subsequent block, a situation that as an effect makes the blocks that preceded the one that was modified cannot be linked again because as a requirement to link in which they must have the identifier of the block that precedes them, generating a drop of all the other blocks in the chain.

to be incorporated into other areas, such as health, law, commerce and even for the democratic electoral processes of each of the states. These systems can be created with certain variations, being able to be a public or permissioned blockchain, the first alludes to the fact that any natural or legal person from anywhere on the planet can be part of the chain, and the clearest example is cryptocurrencies.

As for the permitted systems, these systems basically refer to the fact that their access and participation are restricted to a specific group of people or companies, and in this sense we can highlight the case of the national network Alastria of Spain, which according to Javier Ibáñez [7], "(...) operates on an Ethereum-type network...," in addition to the fact that it uses a concession protocol called Istanbul Byzantine Fault Tolerance (IBFT) that helps self-management to take decisions, in addition to having a verification system called Proof of Authority (POA) and "(...) that allows them to provide crypto services and secure inter-nodal communication..." [11].

Now, it is necessary to treat the Ethereum platform, just as bitcoin also allows you to transfer cryptocurrencies globally, but it is also capable of creating blockchain-based applications, on the Ethereum website, it is mentioned that: "(...) any computer program can run on Ethereum..." [12] opening an infinite number of possibilities for the use of blockchain in fields other than fintech.

As stated above, blockchains were developed at the same time as the creation of cryptocurrencies; however, this is not their only functionality, they have been used to create Non-Fungible Tokens or better known by their acronym (NFT or NFTs) and these files have a unique digital signature and allow you to trade an endless number of digital files, such as images, audios, videos, etc. [13]; there are cases in which pieces of digital art have been traded.

Another form of use of blockchain is found in the Smart Contracts; however, before conceptualizing and analyzing them in detail, it is important to refer to Legal Tech and this concept was used since the "(...) 9s (in) the United States as part of the fintech phenomenon with which it has obvious connections to the extent that the large firms that require Legal Tech services are providing advisory services in operations and financing projects that, in turn, they systematically employ resources from fintech or advanced financial technology companies..." ([7], p. 117).

In other words, as the world of cryptocurrencies advances, Legal Tech also does so, as it also helps to guarantee certain types of transactions, but it is not only limited to that, it also seeks to help with advice, consulting, preparation of documents, selection of regulations applicable to each legal case and the preparation of financial documents themselves, among others. In addition, Legal Tech can be used by the justice administration system or its auxiliary agencies, such as notaries, registrars and even by the prosecutor's office.

Now, the Smart Contract concept was originally proposed by Nick Szabo [14]: "(...) A set of promises, including protocols within which the parties perform on the other promises. The protocols are usually implemented with programs on a computer network, or in other forms of digital electronics, thus these contracts are 'smarter' than their paper-based ancestors. No use of artificial intelligence is implied...."

As you may notice in part of its definition, reference is made to the ancestors of this type of Smart Contract, which are written contracts, within the doctrine and in a large part of the civil codes of the Roman tradition, a contract is defined as an agreement or convention by which one party is obliged to another to give, to do or not to do something. A large part of this type of contract is notarized and it is these entities that keep a record of these contracts; however, in case of conflicts due to non-compliance, it can be appealed to a judicial authority, that is, a judge, to order its compliance, failing which we can resort to alternative methods for the resolution of conflicts, such as mediation or arbitration. This is within the Ecuadorian context.

If we realize that they are a series of steps, which take a long time to execute, but in the end they seek to guarantee the full fulfillment of a contractual obligation; in the case of Smart Contracts, they seek to condense all this information into scripts,[2] or lines of code that allow the contract to be automated, and as they are part of a blockchain, a unique identification number is also assigned to each of them. So, its manipulation is prevented. At first, this type of contract was aimed at the transmission of securities in the financial markets of cryptocurrencies.

However, in reality, Smart Contracts have meant, in a way, a series of confusions for the legal world, and we will understand it starting from the following premise: Ethereum as a platform allows the implementation and execution of programs that can be deployed on the Ethereum blockchain, and these programs are created through a programming language called Solidity. Any program created with this programming language began to be called a Smart Contract, a situation that contradicts the definition initially proposed and this is why this term has confused the legal community, since any type of program that establishes a series of conditions for its operation or execution would be considered a Smart Contract, without necessarily there being an obligation between two or more parties.

Hence, Tur Faúndez [9] refers to the fact that several of these Smart Contracts do not necessarily carry some kind of legal relevance, and as an example of this, the most basic of programs is the "HELLO WORLD," which is in a certain way the first step for those who are introduced in a programming language. And on the contrary, there are those contracts that are going to have a legal relevance, and they would be those programs that aim to automate a benefit obligation, but with certain conditions that come from the Ethereum platform, in this case the two parties must have an address on the said platform, which implies having an account on this platform. So, if we lease a property under this modality, then a script must be programmed to automate the payment of that lease.

Although what is achieved is the automation of payment and compliance with it due to the security that blockchain entails, in essence this activity is not as such a legal business, first starting from the fact that we will never be able to observe the contract, these are only lines of code, and second the agreement of wills is dispensed with, of the object, of the cause (lawful) and the most relevant aspect of a contract in the field of law, consent.

With these appraisals, it is undeniable that the ideal name for a contract that must comply with all these characteristics must be considered, and the proposed name is that of smart legal contracts (SLCs), which according to Ferrari [15] "(...) are based on Smart Contract Code but are specifically designed to comply with legal regulations and the needs of the legal system. SLCs rely on blockchain technology and incorporate traditional legal language, thereby ensuring the legal validity of contracts...."

These contracts in turn are structured to be able to comply with certain requirements including the identification of the parties, putting the conditions of the contract in writing and above all the consent and acceptance of the conditions by each of the parties, another characteristic is that this type of contract will not necessarily be part of the blockchain, they can simply be used as a digital tool.

Smart legal contracts are very different from Smart Contracts, and it should be noted that the former have their basis or support not only in a programming language,

[2] It is a set of instructions that are executed to automate routine tasks.

but also in the legal field applicable to the specific case; we can also talk about controversies in the fulfillment of the contract, in the case of smart legal contracts, these allow both delaying their execution and modifying the conditions in order to meet the needs of the parties, and on the other hand, Smart Contracts do not allow the flexibility of the conditions, if the condition is not met, the contract is not terminated.

A significant characteristic of smart legal contracts is that in order to interact with the real world, they must make use of a mechanism called oracles. This is because they lack the ability to access external data, so there are several types of oracles based on software, hardware or also humans; software users have a built-in database that allows them to collect information from the network and then transmit it to the contract, those that are hardware-based take information from the real world to incorporate it into the contract, it can be the case of use of sensors, and finally humans who basically use cryptography to incorporate information into the contract, being the most risky and inaccurate.

We can then end this section by indicating that the blockchain is a database that allows us to guarantee the integrity and invulnerability of information that becomes part of the chain by assigning identifiers that are very difficult to manipulate. We also have smart legal contracts that allow us to have documents that are supported by the law, to guarantee the validity of the agreements agreed between two or more people, and which can be part of the blockchain.

3.2 Artificial intelligence (AI)

The term artificial intelligence (AI) was first coined by scientist John McCarthy[3] in 1956 during what was called the Dartmouth Conference, defining it as "(...) the science and engineering of making intelligent machines, especially intelligent computer programs..." [11].

A whole spectrum against and in favor has been developed on this definition, terrifying thousands due to the unfounded fear of a possible rebellion of machines and enslavement of humans, an aspect that has been covered too much by science fiction, but it has also made us dream of things that we thought impossible. And without going too far with expectations, today we are surrounded by artificial intelligence, which helps us with our daily tasks, such as voice assistants (Siri, Alexa, Cortana, etc.) that allow us to make calls, shopping lists, reminders and more. AI has even been developed that understands our language and can answer multiple questions, such as the AI models applied by OpenAI through ChatGPT, among a myriad of other AIs that currently exist.

Google [16] tells us that artificial intelligence, "(...) is a field of science related to the creation of computers and machines that can reason, learn and act in a way that would normally require human intelligence or that consume data whose scale exceeds what people can analyze...."

As we can see, artificial intelligence has become the central axis of innovation in modern computing; however, we cannot understand it without emphasizing two concepts that are intimately related to AI, and these are Machine Learning and Deep Learning, the first is a concept that is even somewhat older than the ideation of AI itself. Because what is sought through Machine Learning is that machines learn, with small amounts of information, to do things, in that sense it is considered as a subset of artificial intelligence and there are three classes [16]:

[3] Pioneer in the field of artificial intelligence (AI).

i. Supervised learning: It consists of providing structured or labeled data, so that the result is what we have specified. So if we want the AI to recognize images of cats, we must provide it with images of cats; the drawback with this method is that it depends on human intervention to provide such structured data and thus correct and make the AI learn.

ii. Unsupervised learning: Here, labeled data are not provided, and what is sought is for AI to learn to recognize patterns. Here, the human is not needed for its intervention, but AI learns to classify information on its own.

iii. Reinforcement learning: Basically, it is summarized in learning by doing, in this case a series of trial-and-error experiments are applied, receiving reinforcement or rewards in case of achieving a positive result.

Deep Learning, on the other hand, is a subset of Machine Learning, which uses a network of artificial neurons to process and analyze huge amounts of information. It is called Deep Learning because it consists of many layers of analysis, and it is these layers that are responsible for each of the factors that make up the different decisions of the system [17]. This type of learning is present in a large part of the tasks that today resemble AI.

Now, it is necessary to talk about the use of IAs in the practice of law, the functions of IA are not yet focused as such on the elaboration or structuring of legal arguments, but focus on tedious tasks, such as document review, and focus on more common activities.

Without a doubt, the documentary review is one of the most complicated and time-consuming tasks carried out by a lawyer, from sentences, to an infinity of doctrine, a part of IA has been dedicated to facilitating this arduous work that helps to perfect arguments and defense strategies. This is how with a supervised learning model, certain IAs have been trained to recognize legal documents and then with the unsupervised model they are taught to recognize specific parts of those documents.

In this way, these IAs can extract specific information from a document reviewed by them, and in other slightly more complex systems, it has even been possible to detect which parts of that document may constitute an argument for or against certain subjects. Another of the applications and which was only enunciated in previous lines is the search for precedents, and in this field the Americans have a clear advantage because they have been able to train AI to answer specific questions with the search for precedents, making use of natural language, something like what ChatGPT does but which focuses specifically on the judicial system.

Another aspect in which AI has innovated is the implementation of chatbots for legal assistance, and that helped solve small doubts about certain issues, and in this case again the Americans have an advantage, although little by little we see how these methods are beginning to be implemented in other countries.

Something that deserves a lot of importance is that the legal sector is in a certain way conservative and has sought to preserve its forms for a long time, and here it deserves special emphasis to refer to the situation that both the system of administration of justice and its auxiliary bodies are going through, such as notaries, registries, prosecutor's office, etc. That it is very difficult for it to implement these tools of the new digital era, and they mostly respond to the great economic challenge of creating a system to digitize and automate a large part of legal work.

Although there are platforms that facilitate the consultation of cases, mandatory jurisprudential precedents and procedural actions, they are very far different from the platforms that are developed based on AI, and as for the specific issue of notaries, this has presented slight changes in the last 20 years; however, all their activity continues to be maintained in physical presence, and it is not possible to corroborate or consult online, we must physically go to a notary's office if we want to consult a notary regarding a contract or document.

3.3 The notary's office as a digital platform, with the application of artificial intelligence (AI)

Once we have understood what a blockchain, smart legal contracts and artificial intelligence (AI) entail, we must talk about the scenario that can allow us to revolutionize the notarial system in Ecuador, as a background we must state that notaries have more than 200 years guaranteeing and providing security and certainty to contracts, wills, agreements, promises, etc. Notaries are responsible for giving public faith to these documents.

Public faith is a legal presumption regarding the veracity made by competent and upright officials to whom the law empowers to imbue certain instruments with certainty [18]. In other words, it is to certify the authenticity and legitimacy of a document, and this act in certain cases constitutes a substantial solemnity for its full validity.

With the appearance of blockchain and smart legal contracts, we could understand that in a certain way the figure of the notary could be dispensed with; however, this is nothing more than an *Ad populum*[4] fallacy product of the immutability and security that blockchain poses, but it is enough to review what has happened in the case of notaries in Spain, who have made it clear that this kind of digital notary formulated by the blockchain only poses a challenge for the Anglo-Saxon notary and not for Latin notaries [6], or in other words, it does not entail a complication for notaries of the Roman tradition, and this is basically due to the fact that a large part of the notarial codes and laws provide for both the verification of certain requirements in contracts and other actions such as the protocolization and physical registration of these actions, a task that in the Ecuadorian case is still done physically.

In this sense, we could not talk about the replacement of the figure of the notary or even a possible disappearance of the notary, in a strict sense, what would result from the implementation of a digital notarial platform would be an update of the functions that the notary historically performs, with the support of new technologies, because in the future we could see a decentralized notarial system, in which each of the nodes of this network are the notaries themselves and other collaborators authorized to belong to the said network, that is, to create a decentralized and permissioned digital platform.

Although this would be a great leap for notaries, the implementation of these technologies would have a greater impact and benefit for the users of the notarial system, since the authenticity and legitimacy provided by the notary would be more supported by the immutability and security that the blockchain can provide; however, it is a gigantic challenge, as it would imply the digitization of hundreds of documents, apart from the creation of such a system.

---

[4] A Latin phrase that refers to a type of fallacious argument that purports to make a claim based solely on the fact that many people believe it to be so.

Now, it is necessary to address the issue of artificial intelligence in the notarial system, and in that sense, we could start from the smallest, that is, from supervised Machine Learning to unsupervised to train AI to recognize legal documents and be able to differentiate between the different structures of the clauses, and thus advance to Deep Learning that allows handling a vast amount of information. This for the IA to learn to establish what type of clauses presents incompatibilities for the full execution of the contract or that could represent a risk for the parties involved in a legal transaction.

This would facilitate the verification of requirements that our own law provides, as stated in Articles 27 of the (Ecuadorian) Notarial Law "(...) Before drawing up a public deed, the notary must examine: 1 The capacity of the grantors; 2 The freedom with which they proceed; 3 The knowledge with which they are bound; and, 4 If the tax and municipal rights to which the act or contract is subject have been paid. The omission of this duty shall have no other effect than the fine imposed by law on the notary..." [3].

These tasks that can be considered tedious, repetitive and that also take up a large part of the time of notaries, which could be addressed by artificial intelligence, being necessary to have access to other databases such as those of the different municipalities and tax collecting entities, as we see this does not necessarily mean that the notary should cease to exist, rather, it should continue to be present, since there may be cases in which the AI algorithm does not filter these parameters well and the notary can intervene to even improve the development and learning of the IA, this would mean that the notary must have minimum knowledge of the operation of the IA to make such corrections.

The future of technology seems to change day by day, and both blockchain and AI are undergoing transformations and advances by leaps and bounds, so in the last 4 years it has been possible to observe how they have had a great impact on daily activities, the notary has been an essential part of many states, and it is undoubtedly one of the sectors of the legal world, which most likes to maintain its use and forms.

However, that is what is causing a delay in relation to the undeniable technological advances that we see today, to show a button, at present in the Ecuadorian judicial system, it is no longer necessary to physically go to file a brief, we can do it through platforms that facilitate this work. But notaries' offices are still a space that does not have this ease of access, you must go physically to carry out any procedure.

And part of the change could start there, not necessarily implement a digital system of decentralized architecture, we could try as Spain did at the time with the SIGNO platform[5] that interconnected Spanish notaries and created a database that facilitated communication and even the acquisition of notarial services. Copying is not always bad, and even more so when it involves a radical change for the benefit of society.

3.4 Challenges and limitations of the application of artificial intelligence to the Ecuadorian notarial system

At first, it is necessary to state that we should not be scandalized by an apocalyptic future where AI enslaves humanity or condemns us to extinction. This point, although irrelevant and perhaps without any purpose, must be addressed because there are many people who take this apocalyptic scenario as something inevitable. However, it is nothing more than a science fiction myth.

[5] Acronym that refers to the Integrated Notarial Management System, a centralized architecture system that makes use of a virtual private network (VPN).

In this regard, it should be noted that the learning process of an IA is limited to the type of information provided to it and the purpose for which that IA is developed, and in a strict sense, it is somewhat unlikely that a scenario will arise in which the IA represents a potential risk to humanity. However, as for the specific object of this article, the doubt that would arise would be whether the IA can replace the notarial service and the people involved in the process, and the truth is that it cannot.

Although there is talk of the automation of certain functions, the notarial system due to its way of being and the relevance it has for society, it will not be able to be fully automated, which would mean that there will not be a significant reduction in the staff working in a notary's office. As mentioned in previous lines, AI can perform much more complex, systematic and abundant information processing than a human, and the objective of the implementation of this technology would be to simplify the tasks carried out by a notary's office.

The biggest challenge that this type of technology has encountered in Ecuador is its implementation, since it would be necessary to create this entire system from scratch, which implies a large expenditure of economic resources by the State, but which, without a doubt, would be done for the benefit of the citizens who are in the end the main user and beneficiary of the notary system.

Rivero Ortega ([5], p. 71) refers to the fact that: "(...) The answer to the question of whether bots can take over tasks from public employees is unequivocally positive, but very different is the question of whether it is lawful to allow them to do so in any case..." a comment with which we agree, because those who are called upon to watch over this situation are the legislators of each of the different countries, and it is they who must seek for the rights of people and in this case prevent humans from being replaced in public service.

4. Discussion of results

This research deepened the understanding of blockchain technology and smart legal contracts, indicating how these innovations can be leveraged in the Ecuadorian notarial field. Theoretically, we established that smart legal contracts are not simple Smart Contracts but must comply with legal requirements to be considered valid contracts within the legal framework of any state. This solves the conceptual confusion between Smart Contracts and smart legal contracts. Finally, this research analyzed how artificial intelligence can be applied in notarial tasks, which opens new conceptual perspectives on the interaction between technology and the traditional notarial function.

Well, it is imperative to determine that from the practical field the present research essay formulates a concentrated idea of a decentralized notarial digital platform, based on the study of all the literature on the components that should be implemented in this digital platform, such as blockchain technology, smart legal contracts and, above all, AI. Therefore, the conceptualizations, uses and benefits of these technological components have been addressed throughout this work. These ideas, which are the first steps for the digitization of notarial processes, would make it possible to speed up and simplify procedures for users of notarial activities, which is precisely what technology seeks, to provide benefits to human beings.

Likewise, in summary, this research seeks to offer an important preliminary contribution of ideas in a theoretical and practical spectrum, with the clear objective that in the future it can be revolutionized in Ecuadorian notarial practice, taking advantage of the benefits and capabilities generated by new information technologies, such as: blockchain, smart legal contracts and artificial intelligence, emphasizing, as has already been said in the preceding lines, to benefit the life of the human being.

5. Conclusions

Blockchain, with its ability to ensure the integrity and invulnerability of data through unique and difficult-to-manipulate identifiers, offers a robust and reliable system for various applications, including smart legal contracts. These Smart Contracts not only automate processes, but also incorporate essential legal elements, such as party identification and consent, ensuring their validity within the legal framework. By combining the inherent security of blockchain with legal compliance, smart legal contracts represent a significant evolution in the way contractual agreements are managed and executed, adapting to a digital environment without losing sight of the need to comply with the law.

Artificial intelligence (AI), since its conception in 1956, has evolved exponentially, becoming a fundamental component of modern technology. Its influence extends from everyday applications, such as voice assistants, to specialized fields such as law, where it is transforming complex processes, such as document review and the search for judicial precedents. Despite its growing adoption, especially in countries such as the United States, the legal sector still faces significant challenges in implementing AI, due to its conservative nature and economic barriers to digitalization. However, AI continues to advance, and its integration into the judicial system promises to revolutionize new possibilities to improve efficiency and accuracy in the practice of law.

The digital transformation of notaries' offices, through the application of technologies, such as blockchain and artificial intelligence (AI), promises to revolutionize the notarial system in Ecuador and in other parts of the world. Although the idea of replacing the notary with these technologies is misguided, their integration could significantly improve efficiency and security in the management of legal documents. The creation of a decentralized digital notarial platform and the implementation of AI for tasks, such as the verification of contractual clauses and the authentication of documents, are steps toward a future in which notarial work is modernized, maintaining its relevance in society. However, this change presents enormous challenges, especially in the digitization of records and in the need for notaries to acquire basic knowledge about the operation of these new technologies. As blockchain and AI continue to advance, it is crucial that the notary sector embraces these innovations so as not to be left behind in the digital age, ensuring that notaries remain instrumental in validating and legitimizing documents, but with improved efficiency and accessibility for users.

Finally, we must be honest as authors of this research work, that artificial intelligence (AI) is a great digital tool that is quite helpful in the various fields of daily life. The living example of this is that we come from a Spanish-speaking country, although we handle the English language and understand it, in this work we use the benefits of AI, so that writing in English is as technical as possible, therefore, this same research essay is proof of the advantages that the use of AI entails, it is essential to adapt to the new changes that technology brings with it.

Author details

Luis Eduardo Rengifo Aispur[1,2,3,4*] and Freddy Patricio Torres Briones[1,5]

1 Private Practice, Latacunga, Ecuador

2 Courts of the Republic of Ecuador, Universidad Autónoma Regional de los Andes [UNIANDES], Ambato, Ecuador

3 Law with a Focus on Administrative Law, Universidad Autónoma Regional de los Andes [UNIANDES], Ambato, Ecuador

4 Procedural Law and Oral Litigation, Universidad Internacional SEK [UISEK], Quito, Ecuador

5 Courts of the Republic of Ecuador, Universidad Central del Ecuador, Quito, Ecuador

*Address all correspondence to: luis.edu0027@gmail.com

References

[1] Oppenheimer A. Every Man for Himself. Spain: Debate; 2018

[2] Gómez A, Faerna M. The Role of the Notary in the European Union. 2nd ed. Spain: Europa Nihil Prius Fide Notario - Colegios Notariales de España; 1999

[3] Notarial Law, Ecuador, Published in Official Gazette No. 158 on November 11, 1966

[4] Díaz D. Notarial Practice Manual. Ecuador: Corporación de Estudios y Publicaciones - CEP; 2013

[5] Rivero Ortega R. Derecho e Inteligencia Aritifical. Spain: Olejnik; 2023

[6] Fernández-Bravo L, Francés et al. Legal Tech and notarial function. In: Andrés MB, editor. Legal Tech. The Digital Transformation of the Legal Profession. 2nd ed. Spain: LA LEY Soluciones Legales, SA; 2023. pp. 653-694

[7] Ibáñez JJ. Blockchain and Legal Tech. In: Barrio Andrés M, editor. Legal Tech. The Digital Transformation of the Legal Profession. 2nd ed. Spain: The Law; 2023. pp. 111-124

[8] Zhabina A. Chinese court already solves cases with artificial intelligence. Deutsche Welle. Technology. 2023. Available from: https://www.dw.com/es/las-cortes-de-china-ya-utilizan-inteligencia-artificial-para-resolver-casos/a-64471873

[9] Tur FC. Smart legal contracts. In: Barrio Andrés M, editor. Legal Tech. The Digital Transformation of the Legal Profession. 2nd ed. Spain: The Law; 2023. pp. 144-159

[10] Hernández Sampieri R et al. Metodología de la investigación. 6th ed. México: Editorial Mc Graw-Hill/ Interamericana Editores, S.A; 2014

[11] Government of Spain [Internet]. Recovery, Transformation and Resilience Plan. Available from: https://planderecuperacion.gob.es/noticias/que-es-inteligencia-artificial-ia-prtr#:~:text=que%20posteriormente%20McCarthy%20definir%C3%ADa%20como,encuentra%20en%20la%20ciencia%20ficci%C3%B3n; [Accessed August 20, 2024]

[12] Ethereum [Internet]. ethereum.org. Available from: https://ethereum.org/es/learn/; [Accessed August 20, 2024]

[13] Kaspersky [Internet]. AO Kaspersky Lab. Disponible en: https://latam.kaspersky.com/resource-center/definitions/what-is-an-nft?srsltid=AfmBOorsqJXwcxAA5bUx_Jy2WIwpv85HMfiI_yUPH1cpwp-zO65bbR15; [Consultado Agt 20, 2024]

[14] Szabo N. Uva.nl [Internet]. Disponible en: https://www.fon.hum.uva.nl/rob/Courses/InformationInSpeech/CDROM/Literature/LOTwinterschool2006/szabo.best.vwh.net/smart_contracts_glossary.html [Consultado Agt 20, 2024]

[15] Ferrari D. MEDIUM [Internet]. Disponible en: https://medium.com/@davide.ferrari/smart-legal-contract-slc-smart-contract-code-scc-c53b318323cb [Consultado Agt 20 2024]

[16] Google [Internet]. Google Cloud. Available from: https://cloud.google.com/discover/

deep-learning-vs-machine-learning; [Accessed August 20, 2024]

[17] Gómez SS. Artificial intelligence. In: Andrés MB, editor. Legal Tech. The Digital Transformation of the Legal Profession. 2nd ed. Spain: LA LEY Soluciones Legales, SA; 2023. pp. 126-142

[18] Bernal Ordóñez M et al. Notarial Law Practice. 1st ed. Colombia: Editorial Nomos S.A; 2018

Chapter 6

The Right Prescription: The Digital Transformation of the Department of Drug Control and Food Administration (DC & FA) in Tamil Nadu, India

Arpan Subhashis Barik, Karunakaran Zachariah, Ajith Asha, Appadurai Karthik and Ganesan Kannan

Abstract

The Department of Drug Control & Food Administration (DC & FA), Government of Tamil Nadu, in India, established in 1981 is responsible for regulating the manufacture and sale of drugs and cosmetics in the State of Tamil Nadu. The department, until recently, processed all received applications manually, with the requirement of license seekers to physically submit the requisite documents at designated Citizen Service Centres (CSCs)/designated counters within the department premises itself. Naturally, this had led to inordinate challenges for the department as well as businesses, especially retail pharmaceutical outlets. Given the challenges faced by the DC & FA and similar state agencies, beginning in 2020, an end-to-end digitization initiative of 200+ services was pioneered by Guidance, the nodal agency for investment promotion for the State of Tamil Nadu. This resulted in enhancing accessibility, reducing cost, and increasing efficiency of the licensing process. This chapter explores the eventful journey that led to the successful implementation of the system, by using aggregate quantitative statistics and in-depth qualitative consultations with the department and licenses. As a result of this initiative, small retailers now have access to easy, transparent, entirely digital licensing, which democratizes the significantly improve the interface between government and business.

Keywords: digitization, government-to-business, citizen services, digital transformation, drug manufacturing license, drug retail license, one stop portal, investments, doing business, E-governance, economy, transaction cost, public value

1. Introduction

The Alma-Ata declaration emphasizes that medicines play a crucial role in primary health care [1]. Access to medicines [2] is crucial not just to save lives and promote health but to prevent epidemics and diseases too [3]. This assumes significance in India given the size and spread of the population. In India, pharmacies (Medicine Stores) complement the public health system in improving the access to medicines, given that all drugs sold in India are Over-the-Couter (OTC) unless specified otherwise, requiring a prescription. Given the criticality of pharmacies on realizing the public health goals of the State and ensuring a healthy populace, as well as the need for robust quality control on products, the manufacturing, storing, and selling of drugs is comprehensively regulated by the Drug Control Authority of the respective States. The Department of Drug Control & Food Administration (DC & FA), Government of Tamil Nadu is responsible for regulating the Drugs manufacturing and distribution to >70 million people spread across 38 Districts (Administrative Divisions followed in India and within the State of Tamil Nadu). The Department is involved in the provision of 30–40 related licenses to Drug Retailers and Manufacturers such as the grant for manufacturing allopathic/schedule x drugs, wholesale/retail license for allopathic drugs, test licenses, grant of WHO-GMP certifications to name a few critical licenses. The State is home to >50,000 pharmacies and > 60,000 registered pharmacists.

Given the context, the centrality of the DC& FA in regulating, administering, and managing the drug and pharmaceutical ecosystem in Tamil Nadu can be noted.

2. Understanding the challenge

Under the erstwhile practice of licensing, the department had followed two methods of granting approvals/licenses. The first method required those requiring approvals/licenses to physically visit the department and submit the required documentation along with the application and concerned fees to a dedicated desk manned by the concerned officials. The second method involved leveraging a hybrid mechanism (comprising online and physical interfaces) run by a third party, wherein the applicants had to visit the Common Service Centre for citizens (termed as E-Sevai Centre-Sevai being the local word for 'help'), submit the requisite documents to the data entry operator who would fill the application on behalf of the applicant, and collect the stipulated fees. To initiate and complete this process, the applicants had to often travel great distances to the nearest centre (sometimes 80–100 KMs). There are 14,000 such E-Sevai Centres spread across the State of Tamil Nadu.

Numerous pharmacies and industry associations raised the inordinate challenges faced in the course of procuring the requisite licenses including the presence of physical touchpoints, large manpower costs involved in the process, changing documentation requirements, technical glitches at the CSCs necessitating multiple visits, among others. Furthermore, the data entry operator at the E-Sevai Centre often used his/her mobile number at the time of the filing applications, thereby leading to the dependency of applicants on the data entry operator to track the status of their respective applications. All these challenges stymied the retail pharmaceutical sector from complying with regulatory requirements, increasing the regional presence, and obtaining periodic compliances/renewals in a timely manner, thereby affecting the ease and access to over-the-counter drugs and medication for the general public. Recognizing the criticality of providing access to medicines [1], the Government of India has also pioneered critical initiatives such as launching Jan Aushadhi Stores to enable access to quality and affordable medicines with high-quality control measures [4]. In light of the pressing context, there arose an urgent need to democratize the entire licensing process and simplify the business interface, while ensuring quality and supply of medicines to the population.

3. Literature review

As pointed out by theorists, digital transformation initiatives empower the citizens / businesses to access their rights / services and enable Governments to create new capability [5] and improve their performance / efficiency [6]. Increasing efficiency of these Government organizations / institutions are expected to improve the service delivery as well as provide work relief to the officers within the public institutions allowing them to focus on more qualitative aspects of service delivery [7]. Digital initiatives do not just impact accessibility and quality of public services but affect the way other functions (such as policy making, regulations, enforcement, and administration) are performed. A key point raised by some authors has been that prior studies on digitization have focused on the availability of services, rather than the quality, ease, and efficiency aspects of the same [8]. This aspect lends credence to our proposed study, as well as future studies on the topic. As pointed out by authors such as Douglas North, there is also a perennial need to lower transaction costs in every economic interaction to ensure that the general welfare of the target group is never undermined in the face of vested interests, bureaucratic or political [9]. Building on the findings of the digitization journey of Tamil Nadu [10], the objective of this study is to assess the impact of digitization on a particular public sector institution and the public value it creates on the specific target group. Underscoring this digital initiative, the role of the same in reducing transaction costs [9] and solving information asymmetry is also central to understanding the larger perspective. Experts have also pointed to the long-term impact of digitization initiatives, which enable governments to 'govern' more effectively, while increasing efficiency and reducing wait-time [11].

Using this framework, the study attempts to analyze and measure the impact of digitization initiatives on businesses/citizens and administration and identify success factors and challenges related to such initiatives, along the parameters of time, cost, accessibility, reliability, and transparency.

The findings are expected to inform theoretical and practical considerations in the implementation of digitization initiatives by public agencies in other regions of India, and extendable to similar economies across the world.

4. Department transformation exercise

The Department of DC & FA administers its services through a Head Office at Chennai (the Capital city), headed by a director, operating through 25 zonal offices headed by assistant directors covering the 38 Districts in the State of Tamil Nadu.

In addition to these officers, the Drug Control Inspectors, who are based out of the head office and each zonal office, play a pivotal role in conducting on-site inspections and issuing inspection reports.

As a part of the larger digitization transformation exercise spearheaded by guidance (the nodal agency for investment promotion and facilitation in the State) under the aegis of the State Industries Department, digitization 200+ Government to Business (G2B) services spanning across 40+ Government Departments were initiated in the year 2020 [10]. These included 30+ services of the Department of DC & FA. Given that the Department accounts for more than 90% of the 40,000 applications received [12] on Tamil Nadu Single Window Portal (TNSWP), it was selected for the purpose of this study.

As a first step to ensure a governance mechanism for the larger digitization initiative and to provide legislative backing to the larger digitization initiative, amendments to 'The Tamil Nadu Business Facilitation (Act & Rules) (TNBFAR), 2017-18' were made to mandate accepting and processing of applications for these 200+ services (including the services of the DC & FA) in a fully digitized manner. The TNBFAR 2017–18 also covered the stipulated timelines for grant of licenses, monitoring mechanisms, punitive measures for non-compliance, and document checklists for the respective services. Through this critical step, the various licensing services/approvals offered by the DC & FA were bolstered.

For the services of the Department of DC & FA, based on the assessment of the current level of automation of the processes, complexity of the forms/document checklist, fee logic, a 'To-be' process flow was developed. This was complemented by consultation with the small businesses who accessed these services on a regular basis. The final concurrence on the proposed process flows for each service/license was obtained from the Department of DC & FA, and the go-ahead was given to the technological Partner for software/system development. The timeline for the development of each service was estimated to be 45 days.

Following the development of the required services, the User Acceptance Testing (UAT) was held with the DC & FA, and following the live deployment, training sessions were held for the process owners (officers) within the Department to familiarize them with the new processes. The user credentials for all officials along with user manuals and video walkthroughs were developed to guide business owners, familiarize them with the new processes, and help them navigate the new system.

5. Research methodology and sampling

To assess the overall impact of the digitization initiative, a *cross-sectional study design* was employed for the study covering the license holders and Department officials. To gauge the impact of the service on the end users, the study covers the users of the TNSWP and the earlier hybrid E-Sevai system to understand the differences from the end-user perspective. In order to capture the administrative (service provider) perspective, officers of the Department of DC & FA were also covered in the study.

Details of the sampling are given in **Table 1** and illustrated in the following sections.

Key indicator/theme	Respondent group	Sample size
Impact of the system on Time and Cost variables	E-Sevai System Users	77
	Single Window Portal Users	70
Administrative perspective	Drugs Inspectors	53
	Assistant Directors	10

Table 1.
Sample size.

Out of a universe of users who had used both the systems, seventy-seven (77) users of the erstwhile hybrid system (i.e., E-Sevai system) and seventy (70) users of the new system (i.e., TNSWP), for a particular license service, were selected through a multi-stage sampling methodology. The sample was spread across the 38 districts of Tamil Nadu. From each district, the users were randomly selected for the study. To the possible extent, in each district, equal representation of E-Sevai system users and TNSWP users was ensured. A semi-structured questionnaire was administered to the users through telephonic survey by a third-party agency to capture data from the system users. The questionnaire consisted of both open-ended and closed-ended questions. The questionnaire was designed to capture the following aspects of the users: demographic details, details about the enterprise, application procedure (i.e., applied through TNSWP vs. E-Sevai), time taken for applying, the presence of manual intervention, cost involved, feedback about the online system, issues faced, and overall satisfaction level.

Administratively, the Drug Control & Food Administration (DC & FA) is headed by a Director and the Department caters to the entire State through its zonal offices. Each of these zonal offices is headed by an Assistant Director (AD) and they are assisted by the Drug Inspectors (DIs). All these officers are involved in the licensing process. Therefore, to gauge the administrative viewpoint, 53 Drugs Inspectors (DIs) and 10 Assistant Directors (ADs) were selected using random sampling technique. A semi-structured questionnaire was administered through an online form, and qualitative interviews conducted with three Assistant Directors and the Director to capture a more nuanced perspective. There were separate questionnaires for the ADs and the DIs. The questions captured the following details: demographic details, views about the digitization initiative, the impact of the digitization on their working, effectiveness of the trainings, adequacy of the infrastructure, and support received from the technological partner appointed for the development of the TNSWP.

6. Results and findings

The results of the study, that is, the impact of the digital transformation initiative on both the users, that is, businesses and the administrators have been assessed in this section. The findings for each of the group are presented separately.

6.1 User profile

In both the user profile groups, majority of the respondents were male. In E-Sevai user group, 86% of the respondents were male, and in TNSWP user group, 84% of the respondents were male. The average age of the respondents was 39 in the E-Sevai user group, while for TNSWP user group it was 38 (**Figure 1**).

For the Department respondents, each officer had spent at least year with the Department.

6.2 User perspective

From the perspective of a small business, the impact on time and cost was studied to assess how the introduction of the new TNSWP system changed the user experience, as against the erstwhile E-Sevai hybrid system that was primarily leveraged.

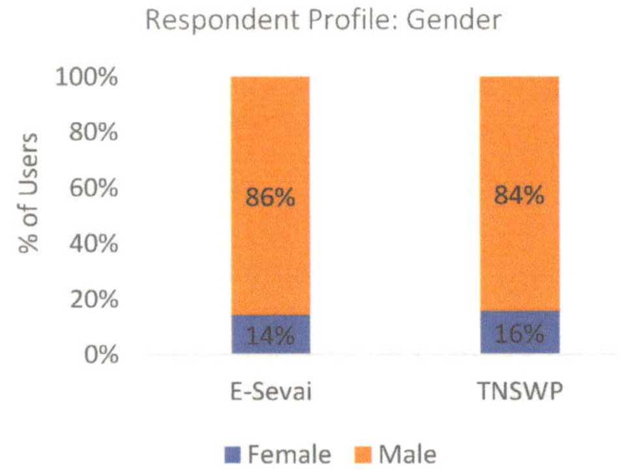

Figure 1.
Gender profile of respondents.

In terms of the time taken to fill up the application, users who leveraged the TNSWP system took 82 Minutes (average time) to fill up the application form, whereas the users who leveraged the E-Sevai system took 59 minutes (average time) as illustrated in **Figure 2** to complete the process. However, users leveraging the E-Sevai system are required to physically travel to a designated E-Sevai Centre. Sixty-six (66%) E-Sevai users said that they had to travel to the E-Sevai Centres/Department for completing the application process and the average additional time involved in visiting the centres was 257 minutes. The time taken for the users leveraging the TNSWP system was higher given that the TNSWP has an additional form that has to be filled by the applicants, that is, the Combined Application Form (CAF), which acts as a common repository form to auto-populate subsequent applications of 25+ Departments with relevant data, if available. However, even though filling the CAF increases the time taken for submitting the initial application through the TNSWP system, the time taken (over numerous applications) for filling additional forms is subsequently reduced. In addition, it may be noted that the TNSWP can be leveraged from any location without the need to physically visit the department concerned.

Though from a process perspective, there was difference in the time required for applying, no major difference were seen in terms of time taken for granting the approval. Seventy-nine percentage of users in each group reported that they had received their approval within the defined timeline by the Department (**Table 2**).

In terms of the cost involved, users who leveraged the E-Sevai system incurred an average additional cost of INR 108 (US$ 1.32) toward travel. The E-Sevai users

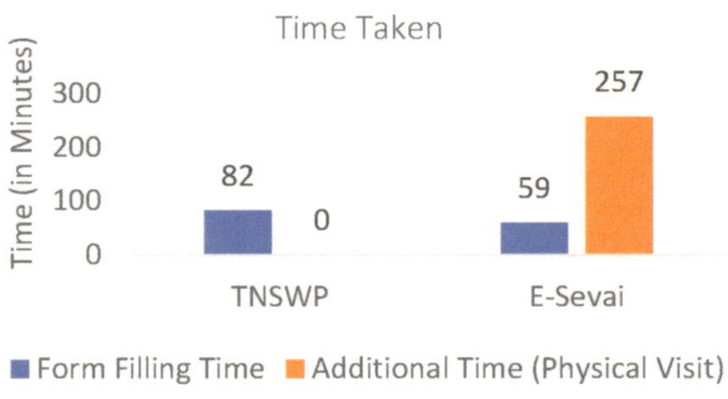

Figure 2.
Time difference for TNSWP users vis-à-vis E-Sevai users.

DOI: http://dx.doi.org/10.5772/intechopen.1007114

Cost component	E-Sevai system user	TNSWP users
Application fees	Yes	Yes
Service charge	Yes	No
Travel cost	Yes	No
Manpower cost (for travel and physical visit)	Yes	No

Table 2.
Difference in type of costs involved for applying for service.

incurred average additional manpower cost of INR 375 (US$ 4.59) as their resources were involved in visiting the department premises or E-Sevai Centre for completing the application process. There was no such expense for users of the TNSWP system.

In addition, one major difference in the cost involved in the E-Sevai Centre, 76 out of 77 E-sevai applicants said that they had paid an average of INR 451 (US$ 5.52) as service charge, whereas there was no such fee levied on TNSWP users.

In terms of the overall ratings, 94% of the E-Sevai users and 88% of the TNSWP users rated the respective system 4 above on a rating scale of 1–5. This difference (higher percentage of E-Sevai users vis-à-vis TNSWP users rating the system 4 and above) can be attributed to difference in the overall process in applying for the service. While in the erstwhile E-Sevai system, a customer service officer present at the E-Sevai Centre is responsible for filling the form and uploading the documents, in the TNSWP system this process has to be entirely done by the applicant. For any assistance in filling the form, the TNSWP user has to take the support of the helpdesk team that assists them virtually. Therefore, continuous efforts are being made by the Department to re-engineer its forms in order to simplify it for the users. The objective is to empower investors so that they do not have to rely on any third-party agents to apply for the service.

6.3 Administrative perspective

From an administrative standpoint, the impact was analyzed from the perspective of process, training, and impact on day-to-day operations for the key personnel involved in the licensing process. In order to understand the process involved in the digitization, we tried to understand the how the leadership drove the new initiative across their team. About 90% (n = 9) of the ADs and 87% (n = 48) said that they learned about the initiative through an official order, duly communicated in the form of a circular from department Head.

6.3.1 Impact of training on officers

As mentioned earlier, frequent trainings/refresher trainings were conducted for all personnel, as and when new services were digitized and deployed online. To assess the impact of training, officers were asked to rate its role in enhancing their ability to leverage the new system, 69% (n = 35) of the DIs and 90% (n = 9) of the ADs rated the training 4 and 5 out of rating scale of 1 to 5.

6.3.2 Impact on working

To understand how the digitization has impacted the officers' work life, specific questions were administered to the ADs and DIs (**Figure 3**).

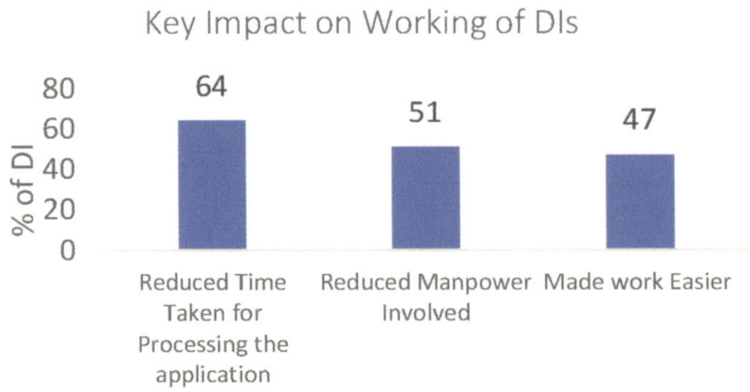

Figure 3.
Impact of digitization on working of DIs.

For the DIs, the reduced time taken to process the application (64%, n = 34), reduced manpower involved (51%, n = 27), and the work made easier (47%, n = 25) were the key impacts highlighted. For the ADs, reduced manpower involved (70%, n = 7) and enabling the officer to focus on other activities such as organizational initiative and learning and development activities (40%, n = 4) were highlighted as the key impacts of this initiative.

However, it is also to be noted that though the system has largely impacted the officers positively as pointed out by 90% (n = 47) of the officers (DIs), there are few 10% (n = 6) who feel that the initiative has not impacted them at all / impacted them negatively.

On probing further for the feedback, it was discerned that there is additional workload given that the working procedure requires uploading the inspection report on the same day, which at times was challenging given the wide geographical coverage. The positive reasons highlighted included the greater transparency built into the licensing process, less paperwork, traceability of the applications, among other key positive outcomes highlighted.

7. Key takeaways / conclusions

In the course of the survey, certain key inputs and learnings emerged. The key takeaways are summarized below:

- *'Champions' matter*: The identification of 2–3 key personnel at various levels of the hierarchy within the department aided in securing the buy-in of critical stakeholders in the process. Communicating the vision and mission of the initiative, coupled with strong champions at every level of the process, aided in transforming the outlook of the department from a paper-based office to a completely digital office in a time span of 3 years.

- *Adoption of intuitive and easy to use on-site technology/tools*: Despite adoption of a digital process, the hesitancy and periodic non-availability or lack of familiarity with handheld devices resulted in inspectors having to return back to the office to upload their inspection reports. Technological adequacy / literacy was identified as not being implemented to the fullest capacity possible, in a uniform manner across districts, thereby leaving scope for improvement.

- *Concurrent gauging of user requirements/inputs*: During entire process of development of the services, end users were the key to the implementation of the system [13]. Numerous entrepreneurs pointed to the urgent need to further simplify the online forms by reducing redundant fields and consequently, it was decided to do this periodically.

- *Staffing, training, and handholding*: A key success factor was the periodic training and handholding support provided by the technological partner to the department officials in parallel with awareness sessions for small businesses. However, given the volume of applications and requirements of uploading inspection/field reports on the same day, it was seen that a greater regional presence would aid in easing the process for the drug inspectors.

- *Dynamic technological adoption*: The services of the department were hosted on the State Single Window Portal on the cloud (Amazon Cloud) using a Java-based platform. Leveraging the latest digital platform technology ensured digital security and a seamless online experience for users of the portal.

From a theoretical perspective, this study reasonably informs the prevailing narrative—that smart digitization and simplification of processes play a critical role in reducing the transaction costs of doing business and significantly ensuring a rise in 'general welfare' of target groups of a particular initiative. This study also provides practical considerations for economies/regions at the cusp if undertaking localized as well as large-scale digital transformation exercises to address inefficiencies in service-provisioning systems. Regions at a similar level of digital maturity and with transferable contexts may stand to benefit from the experiences of this initiative.

8. Limitations and future studies

In conclusion while the administrative and user-centric improvements are evident, the long-term impact of the initiative on achieving larger public health outcomes would require further research.

Further to this, as pointed out earlier this study to a large extent captures the online 'availability' of a service as opposed to a greater detailing of the qualitative aspects of the service. While the focus of this study has predominantly been limited to the impact of digitization on business transformation vis-à-vis erstwhile physical interface-driven systems, it would be worthwhile to undertake further studies on the impact of process re-engineering and rationalization of forms/fields in applications, on the ease of doing business and on economic transactions, from both the administrative and user-centric perspectives.

Acknowledgements

The authors wish to thank the Director of Drug Control & Food Administration Department for extending his support in obtaining user data and offering his inputs from an administrative perspective, M/s. Akara Research and Technologies Pvt. Ltd. for their support in conducting the user survey, and Dr. Devleena Chakravarty for providing her valuable insights for this study.

Author details

Arpan Subhashis Barik[1], Karunakaran Zachariah[2*], Ajith Asha[3], Appadurai Karthik[1] and Ganesan Kannan[4]

1 Deloitte Touche Tohmatsu India LLP, Chennai, India

2 Guidance Tamil Nadu, Chennai, India

3 Government of Tamil Nadu, Chennai, India

4 Drug Control Department Government of Tamil Nadu, Chennai, India

*Address all correspondence to: zachariah@investtn.in

References

[1] World Health Organisation (WHO). 1978. Declaration of Alma Ata. 1978

[2] World Health Organisation (WHO). Equitable access to essential medicines: A framework for collective action. 2004

[3] Kar SS, Pradhan HS, Mohanta GP. Concept of essential medicines and rational use in public health. Indian Journal of Community Medicine. 2010:10-13. Available from: https://www.ncbi.nlm.nih.gov/pmc/articles/PMC2888334/

[4] Singh P, Ravi S, Dam D. Medicines in India: Accessibility, Affordability, and Quality, March 2020. Brookings: India; 2020

[5] Martin A. Digital literacy and the digital society. In: Lankshear C, Knobel M, editors. Digital Literacies Concepts Policies Practices. New York: Peter Lang Publishing; 2008. pp. 151-176

[6] Westerman G, Calmé JC, Bonnet D, Ferraris P, McAfee A. Digital transformation: A roadmap for billion-dollar organizations, MIT Sloan management. MIT Center for Digital Business and Capgemini Consulting. 2011:1-4

[7] Kuhlmann S, Heuberger M. Digital transformation going local: Implementation, impacts and constraints from a German perspective. Public Money & Management. 2021;**43**(2):147-155. DOI: 10.1080/09540962.2021.1939584

[8] Dobrolyubova E. Measuring outcomes of digital transformation in public administration: Literature review and possible steps forward. NISPAcee Journal of Public Administration and Policy. 2021;**14**(1):61-86. DOI: 10.2478/nispa-2021-0003

[9] North DC. Transaction costs, institutions, and economic history. Zeitschrift für die gesamte Staatswissenschaft/Journal of Institutional and Theoretical Economics H. 1984;**1**:7-17

[10] Karunakaran Z, Kulkarni P, Subhashis BA. Paper to cloud: Digitizing the government-to-business (G2B) interface in Tamil Nadu, India. In: Proceedings of the 15th International Conference on Theory and Practice of Electronic Governance (ICEGOV '22). New York, NY, USA: Association for Computing Machinery; 2022. pp. 542-545. DOI: 10.1145/3560107.3560190

[11] Chapple Mike. Digital transformation brings cost savings and private sector quality to government. Available from: https://insights.samsung.com/

[12] Guidance Tamil Nadu. 2022. Single Window Portal dashboard. Retrieved 1 May 2023 from https://tnswp.com

[13] Reynoldson C, Stones C, Allsop M, Gardner P, Bennett MI, José Closs S, et al. Assessing the quality and usability of smartphone apps for pain self-management. Pain Medicine. 2014;**15**(6):898-909. DOI: 10.1111/pme.12327

Chapter 7

Balancing Expectations for Digital Transformation in the Healthcare: Development of the New Cancer Registry in Latvia

Aiga Balode and Ieva Bikava

Abstract

The healthcare sector has been slower to embrace digital transformation compared to other industries. However, it is evident that digitalization offers significant growth and innovation potential, particularly in ensuring patient-centric healthcare. Despite this potential, implementing digital solutions often involves a disproportionately lengthy and challenging process. As an EU member state, Latvia has achieved considerable progress in digitalization, especially in cancer treatment and related data processing. A modern, population-based cancer registry can serve several crucial purposes from both the patient's perspective and in analyzing healthcare quality, cost-effectiveness, service demand, supply, and policy development. Even though digital transformation began over a decade ago, the first phase of national level oncology data management was only implemented in 2024. The key takeaway here is that "Digital Transformation is not merely an IT project!" In the observed case, critical factors influencing success included industry professionals' readiness for change and the active impact of EU initiatives, combining both bottom-up and top-down approaches.

Keywords: digital transformation, healthcare, population-based cancer registry, governance, data management

1. Introduction

Digitalization has been a fundamental cornerstone for transformative changes across various sectors, driving new initiatives and enhancing access to information and services. The healthcare sector has been lagging regarding patient data governance in a systematic and interconnected way, while at the same time being at the forefront of using different new devices for patient treatment, achieving remarkable and even revolutionary progress (one of the remarkable examples—COVID-19 vaccine elaborations). To ensure safe, timely and affordable healthcare services, policymakers nationally and globally stress the importance of digitalization in healthcare, which would foster a swifter transformation of service provision and ensure more timely service availability.

The terms "digitization" and "digitalisation" are interrelated and refer to digital transformation. It is "a process that aims to improve an entity by triggering significant changes to its properties through combinations of information, computing, communication, and connectivity technologies" [1]. The term itself indicates the need to allocate the necessary resources to ensure that envisaged changes take place. As for the healthcare digital transformation, it refers to the adoption of new technologies that enable the shift toward secure, high-quality care and drive greater business efficiency. This definition highlights the expectations that both governments, society, and health professionals expect from digital transformation; however, each digital tool only provides specific improvements and once it is implemented, a new perspective on development is seen.

So, the transformation process is ongoing in the healthcare sector—with the implementation of new digital solutions, technologies and artificial intelligence (AI) options by providing telemedicine services, remote monitoring and maintaining patient records and electronic health records (EHR). All the elements of digital health build a complicated and codependent digital ecosystem where proper governance should be in place for the navigation through all the possibilities to become more efficient.

The pressure for change derives also from international organizations. World Economic Forum (WEF) urges—the healthcare sector needs radical changes to ensure "healthcare for all" and address the healthcare inequities. WEF declares that "delivering on the promise of digital, data and AI in healthcare for improved outcomes will require an ecosystem mentality. No single actor can bring about the digital health renaissance" [2]. This notion corresponds to the concept proposed by the World Health Organization (WHO) that emphasizes the empowerment of citizens (not only patients) and medical staff by involving them more actively and consistently within the digital health development processes. The WHO sees digital health as a key to ensuring universal health coverage that would allow to minimize healthcare inequities, at the same time addressing the urgency to shift toward prevention and personalization of healthcare.

Healthcare systems globally are becoming more expensive and require major changes, shifting away the focus from short-term treatment, toward prevention, health promotion and individualized care [3]. The urge for global healthcare transformation is driven by an aging population and a rise in chronic disease cases when the demand for services continues to grow. Coupled with the slowdown in economic growth, international organizations such as the Organization for Economic Co-operation and Development (OECD), WEF and WHO are calling on countries to standardize data, ensure its exchange and analysis, and develop predictive capabilities for healthcare sector needs and resilience-building scenarios by enlarging and diversifying the collaboration partnerships. This approach aims to facilitate public-private partnerships, making the healthcare sector more adaptable to changes and new initiatives. Ultimately, it seeks to ensure healthcare is a human right, with the individual at the center of the healthcare ecosystem.

As a member of both the EU and international organizations like the OECD and WHO, Latvia has a robust collaboration network and legal framework to implement necessary changes in healthcare. A European Health Data Space (EHDS) strongly advanced by the European Commission brings forward another major homework or shift in the healthcare sector, considering the unequal digital maturity aspects even within one healthcare-providing institution. Nevertheless, it underlines the direction that the EU is taking toward improved services for its citizens.

More dynamic development of digital health is facilitated through digital disruptions that are generally applicable to any other sector [4]. The most known impacting factors are: (1) the fourth industrial revolution—internet of things, smart devices and their interoperability; (2) AI—including automatization of processes, robotization and (3) Big data—modeling and prediction, ensuring self-service options for the end user (like telemedicine, hospitals at home and others). While providing the opportunities, it clearly determines the need for prioritization, systematization and agreed roles and rules for the stakeholders involved. The identified research areas provide little evidence on the digital transformation process itself and governance ensured for the major change management in healthcare. Regarding healthcare, governance applies to infrastructure, architecture, standards and interoperability, and services and applications. It is essential and the main determinant of changes in any sector, often taken for granted and self-explanatory just by having responsible institutions in place. The authors assume that analysis of governance for digital transformation would help to find out the hindering and facilitating factors of healthcare service change and modernization. Given the broad scope of this topic, the authors in this section focus on one specific area of health and healthcare policy: the establishment of a digital population-based cancer register (PBCR). Over the past decade, there has been a dynamic shift from static registers and siloed data sets to data flows, information exchange, and analytics, with significant advancements anticipated through artificial intelligence solutions.

The cancer-beating issues have been a priority for Latvia for the last decade, often escalated on the political agenda by the European Union (EU) and international organizations and very zealously and consistently by patient organizations. The statistical data still indicate the progress necessary for Latvia to reduce the inequities for cancer patients as well as to move toward prevention and early detection. OECD states that "cancer is a major public health concern in Europe" [5]. The OECD health policy study survey highlights how the lack of cancer patient data has been a significant barrier for Latvia, preventing advancements in cancer care. Systematic performance monitoring and improvement depend heavily on data availability. Clinicians have long advocated for the establishment of PBCR to enhance clinical data flows. Additionally, Latvian medical professionals, with their international experience, have been eager to apply their knowledge to patient treatment and actively engage in research and international exchanges to improve patient care.

Both adult clinical university hospitals in Latvia have shown a proactive approach, supported by the Ministry of Health (MoH), by undergoing the accreditation process to establish a center of excellence for cancer treatment and research (OECI accreditation). This initiative has received full backing through EU financial tools, which not only support ICT development but also provide further education for medical staff and aid in the creation of guidelines and algorithms. This effort aligns perfectly with Europe's Beating Cancer Plan, emphasizing its importance on national, international, and public agendas, particularly in terms of access to and development of personalized treatment. MoH determined oncology as one of the main priorities, with the purpose of transforming both the institutional setting, the information flow of data with the available EU supporting mechanisms, and implementing changes for the more effective treatment of patients that would correspond to the WHO and international guidelines. Development in such areas as telemedicine and remote monitoring has been left up to the private-public partnerships implemented by healthcare institutions. Therefore, the focus of this chapter is on the process of the PBCR elaboration as having data in a systematized format is crucial for future developments and thus cannot be postponed or leaped over.

2. The role of PBCR in health care and as a tool in health policy

PBCR is one of the best-known medical registries that provides information on the increase in the life expectancy of a person, as well as the possibilities of rewinding diagnosis and treatment, as a result of which the life expectancy of the population increases, the incidence rate from oncological diseases also increases. PBCR attempts to capture all cases that are related to a specific disease, in this case—cancer, within a defined population. This is an important feature that distinguishes PBCR from other registries—like clinical or hospital registries. As PBCR includes almost all cases within the population, it removes selection bias, which is a usual problem for other registries. Therefore, PBCR is instrumental in the planning and evaluation of disease control programs and the effectiveness of the healthcare system. The role of medical registries "have evolved from calculating basic epidemiological data (incidence, prevalence, mortality) to diverse applications in disease prevention, early diagnosis and screening programs, treatment response, health care planning, decision making and disease control programs" [6].

Population-based registries in which specific data about the patients of determined diseases or conditions are collected and analyzed are the basis for public health, as they provide data on surveillance, inform about the prevalence in the population, as well as provide data on the impact of the disease to population—survival and morbidity. Those registries can also be tools used to evaluate the results of political initiatives and implemented healthcare plans, to cope with the disease by providing appropriate screening, early diagnostics and accessible treatment. One of the most widely used approaches for PBCR besides its main function—is to analyze and evaluate screening program coverage and effectiveness. Mainly it is used for the most widespread cancer types—breast, cervical and colorectal cancers [7]. As concluded by Tucker et al. on analyzing the effectiveness of initiatives "if no substantive changes in cancer incidence rates are observed, it is clear that the interventions are not having an effect," but at the same time pointing out, that "when significant changes in incidence rates are observed, it is rarely possible to ascribe these changes to the implementation of the intervention" [8]. Answering the question: how do those registries accomplish such a wide range of functions? Pop et al. point out that this is achieved by "using a composition of predefined data collection protocols, accessing multiple data sources and collecting the highest possible number of cases from a geographically defined population, doubled by explicit efforts to provide systematic constant data update" [6]. So in turn, the lack of such registries is often mentioned as a hindering factor not only for patient treatment effectiveness but also for policy planning.

Developing the registry is a challenging and complex task, and when initiating the vision and scope of the new registry, as Pop et al. characterize the task: "one should balance the requirements and amount of work required for achieving the objective to the available resources" [6]. Usually, a population-based registry contains data from several sources, data available in EHR, information available in clinical information systems, as well as data from the laboratory tests, such as pathology reports, sometimes genomic tests and gene sequencing reports. As pointed out by Nicholson and Perego—PBCR differs from clinical registries, where the focus is on clinical care, as PBCR collects fewer variables and at less granular detail. As those two registries serve different purposes, it can lead to conflicts "between clinical demands for prognostic precision and epidemiological demands for comparability and completeness" [9]. Of course, the merger of data and interoperability grows with the development of ICT and new digital solutions that challenge the cancer register owners to be alert and have a clear focus on the scope of development, not to be tossed away by the variety of options or too different priorities of target groups.

Collecting different data from different sources to provide a complementary and comprehensive picture of the patients' cases, requires building a multidisciplinary team approach, involving and managing different stakeholders with different expertise and expectations on the registry. That is a time-consuming and labor-intensive process. As pointed out by Nicholson and Perego—"Painstaking commitment is required to ensure the quality of the registry's data" [9]. Weak data quality can be related to undiagnosed cases, uncertainty of diagnoses, under-reporting of cases, inaccurate coding, as well as poor quality of submitted cases, if there is a lack of sufficient and adequate on-board controls.

For an elaboration of the PBCR, the role of stakeholders is significant—medical staff, patients and their representing non-Governmental Organizations (NGOs). For any changes to be successfully implemented, the culture of the institutions plays an important role by providing additional stimulus for improvements. Garmann-Johnson et al. refer to "the Nordic Model" for employee involvement, viewing employees as co-creators in various changes and service implementations. The authors also note a scarcity of articles on employee involvement in digital health transformation. However, three common conditions emerge when involving employees in new idea generation and implementation: access to a broad range of information, full engagement in their work roles, and support from management, which includes allocating time for involvement and ensuring rewards [10]. In the future, it is anticipated that the role of employees will grow to ensure long-term solutions and adapt to necessary changes. The same applies to the involvement of patients.

All that leads to the necessity to build up proper interaction and communication among stakeholders and leadership, which has a clear vision of the results that have to be achieved. As specified by Pop et al.: "Clearly formulated objectives, inclusion criteria, patient outcomes, procedures that cover all the activities of the registry and a properly defined core dataset are mandatory requirements that ensure the fulfillment of the purpose and objective" [6].

According to a literature review on guidelines and recommendations for developing registries, provided by Pop et al., there are several quality influencing factors: governance, information and ethical issues, security and privacy, and last but not least: data quality—that involves two other aspects: data accuracy and completeness. When referencing to specific cancer registry, there are four key aspects mentioned—data quality, comparability, validity, timeliness and completeness [6]. In the authors opinion, interoperability and standardized data exchange have become subsets for the factor "comparability" and should be highlighted also in research.

Living today, in the age of modern technology and providing such various ways of connection through technology and data, another significant factor is to think globally, not only on the local or national level, but much wider. It has been the approach used for clinical research but to ensure the appropriate digital transformation, it has become the necessity of governance well. To fit in the networks established in the EU and globally to beat cancer, there is a need for data harmonization, to provide bases to make data-based decisions. So, when defining the requirements and data sets, to provide the possibility to compare data—there is a need for data standardization and mapping among different local systems and data coding vocabularies, that are used, to provide possibilities to submit national data to international data sets and become a full-fledged partner in international organizations. This task creates the necessity of knowledge and expertise on existing guidelines, standards and existing practice on registry development. To provide interoperability among different systems involved in providing data to PBCR, on national and international levels, according to Nicholson and Perego, the use of data standards is necessary for multiple levels related to IT solutions and involves "address protocols, message formats, document architecture, management of document sharing process, and healthcare terminology" [9].

When developing registries and information systems in the field of healthcare, one should also take into account, that there are some specific rules used for the data exchange among the systems, by using specific data standards. In 1987 specific organization, Health Level 7 (HL7) was established, to provide a "comprehensive framework and standards for the exchange, integration, sharing, and retrieval of electronic health information, that supports clinical practice and the management, delivery and evaluation of health services" [11]. The organization provides specific framework guidelines and standards that are used to exchange information related to healthcare. For decades, a specific standard was used to provide interoperability: Clinical Document Architecture (CDA), and is still used in many solutions over a wide scope. Since May 2012, the new standard "Fast Healthcare Interoperability Resources" or FHIR, has been evolved and is recommended for use in developing new solutions as a next-generation standard framework created by HL7. The use of the new standard contributes, on the one hand, to the creation of modern and sustainable solutions, and on the other hand, this presents new challenges in how to connect data from different systems created and maintained using versions of the previous standard—HL7 CDA.

Issues related to the interoperability of data are connected not only with different technical standards that are used for data exchange: HL7 CDA and HL7 FHIR, but also with the semantic standards—or standards that are used for coding information in different systems. The SNOMED-CT standard, which provides the widest possible glossary of terminology, is increasingly being used in the world. However, its implementation is complex and time-consuming, with the result that only in some countries it is used, and Latvia is not among these Member States. As indicated by Nicholson and Perego: "Given the complex array of healthcare infrastructures and health data systems and the need still to interface with legacy systems, it is unlikely that any single health data standard will solve all the interoperability issues" [9]. Digital literacy and understanding the impact of both technical and substance (sector-specific data sets) standards is crucial for staff to implement digital transformation and have regular improvements possible.

According to the literature review provided by Pop et al. on registry success factors, they are the following: appropriate multidisciplinary team; stable funding; focused aims, data collection systems and functions supporting design, as well as mergeable data, standardized datasets, rules for data collection, experience and expertise on the previously used registration principles, as well as knowledge about patient outcomes [6]. A frequent difficulty, as pointed out by Posadas-Martinet et al., is related to sustainability, to provide "maintenance over time and retaining an organized team of professionals who can guarantee quality and continuity of the records" [12]. To deal with those challenges, the proposed solution is to provide substantial motivation for the main stakeholders, including clinicians and researchers, and even patients, to stimulate the development and continuous improvement of processes and procedures.

Last but not least influencing factor for the successive development of the registry is to provide sustainable and stable funding to develop, and latter—to maintain and expand the registry. The lack of sufficient financial support in the long-term can lead to reluctance to invest and promote the development, as well as have a negative impact on the level of involvement, especially from the clinicians. It leads to an *ad-hoc* or project-based approach that only patches the needs, not building a resilient ecosystem and foundation for long-term development. Also, Tucker et al. point out, that "Perhaps the greatest limitation that can diminish our ability to realize the full potential of PBCR is a lack of funding" [8]. Mery and Bray, more directly and strictly indicated, that "for registries to flourish and become indispensable to public health, governments must first ensure that surveillance is included as part of their overall health plans so that there is a budget for staff and operations" [13]. This statement is based on their research and conclusion, that too often registries are developed based on *ad-hoc* funding, that in some cases even comes from research grants, and that without a sustained budget, the risks of vulnerable registry are very high. The authors indicate the significance of this aspect only increases once taking into account the constant battle for adequate financial resources for healthcare, sometimes requiring choosing between immediate medical help versus long-term governance improvement and DT as the outcome. Therefore, the global cooperation/partnership options are of utmost importance as it is a substantial knowledge transfer tool as well that requires new adjustments.

Although traditional usage of PBCR was related to epidemiological data—nowadays, the usage options of PBCR for other functions or data processing purposes become wider and wider. For example, the development of the approach to use PBCR as a basis for treatment evaluation to analyze the survival of patients who received different treatments. Thus, an ever-increasing role for PBCR is for the patient outcome evaluation, not only using survival data, but also supplementing them with the data on clinical outcomes, and patient-reported outcomes [6, 12]. Adding additional information from clinical information systems, as well as adding data sets from administrative systems, can provide good bases for evaluation of performance indicators and quality assurance measurements. The arising involvement of patients to provide data on treatment evaluation in healthcare is also related to the approach moving toward value-based healthcare. Another use-case for using PBCR registries is studies of quality of life (QoL) for cancer survivors. Studies of QoL can inform on the long-term effects and risk factors related to cancer survivors, with the aim to design interventions to improve QoL for that group of patients, thus improving patients' well-being. For these studies, PBCR is used as a sampling frame and the source of patients to enroll in studies of QoL. Those benefits—the database with patients, to enroll in the study, as mentioned by Thong et al., can be done only in case the patient has been allowed to contact to them in research purposes [14]. Unfortunately, most of PBCR built for epidemiological reasons do not collect the information on the possibility to contact the patient and does not provide the contact information. Here stems another need for in-depth research (not covered by this article) on user experience and user involvement in ICT and digital solution development.

Another direction, that has been observed in the development of registries, is closer cooperation with therapy providers, to supplement existing PBCR data with additional information, which can improve and promote data for clinical trials. It might also help to lessen the administrative burden and exclude duplication of data processing. In those cases, registries can also serve as platforms for patient enrollment and recruitment [6]. The development of precision medicine, which is rapidly developing especially in the field of oncology, demands other data sets and information—linkage with the biobanks, to improve research possibilities in genomics.

As characterized by Tucker et al., PBCR "provide a critical framework that can elevate the science of cancer research." As those registries can provide a population-based sample frame, that can solve the problems associated with external validity or as authors wrote, those registries "make it possible for investigators to obtain a set of case records that truly represent the entire underlying population" [8]. One such case, is the example of a combination of EHR records and PBCR records. In this case, PBCR can be used as a tool to analyze and improve the validity of research by using data from EHR, and linking records of those two systems, each of them initially built up for a different purpose. As pointed out by Thompson et al., "there is tremendous potential to leverage the value gained from integrating EHR and PBCR data for research" [15]. As the PBCR provides in-depth data on oncology diagnostics and tumor characteristics, as well as basic data about the cancer-related treatment, while EHR contains much broader clinical data on the patients. The main gain from those complementary database usage for research is to deal with the selection bias that can arise if using only EHR records.

There is also a place for critique on PBCR, and one of the most common arguments relates to the time delay—the time frame when the data is submitted, analyzed and made available from such registries. Usually, the root of the problem is that data are submitted to the registry in a separate process, and by manually entering data into specific forms. However, new technologies and technical standards, that improve data architecture provide more structured data and are coded to the same semantic standards, thus creating opportunities to automate processes and improve possibilities to submit data to registries. One example of automation, provided by Tucker et al., is the use of NLP methods and algorithms implemented in clinical pathology laboratories, with the aim to obtain cancer patient data for PBCR from pathology reports at the time when the cancer patient is diagnosed based on pathology report [8].

Summing up, it is expected that classical PBCR with the data on epidemiology, can be developed and expanded for other data processing purposes and use cases and functions. However, those additional benefits can become the challenges and cause of countless problems, when formulating requirements of the new register. As there are so many stakeholders and so many additional functions and use cases that demand different data sets and policies, governance and ownership are important for implementation. As said by Mery and Bray: "Strong leadership to oversee and nurture the development of registry is vital to achieve high quality data" [13]. Leadership is considered along with timely communication in all PBCR development and maintenance stages.

3. The reasons behind the need for the digital transformation of PBCR in Latvia

Latvia is a country in the Baltic region of Northern Europe, with a population of 1,871,882 people at the beginning of 2024 [16]. The Cancer Registry of Latvia was established in 1993 by the Oncology Center of the Riga East Clinical University Hospital (RECUH). Later, in 2009, it was relocated to the Center for Disease Prevention and Control (CDPC). Since 2018, responsibility for the register has been shared between the National Health Service (NHS)—which is responsible for the IT solution (according to the GDPR—data processor), and the CPDC—which is responsible for the methodology, data processing, and analysis (according to GDPR—data controller). The previous update on the data fields collected in the registry, as well as changes in methodology for the data collection and entry, was in 2016. At that time, the data entry form for the registry became a part of the National Unified Health Information System, and two updated forms were approved: the Oncology Patient Registration Card and the Oncology Patient Treatment Card [17].

Although the general understanding of the role of PBCR is that its data is the cornerstone of cancer control, enabling the planning, monitoring and evaluation of preventive activities and cancer care, unfortunately, the Cancer Registry of Latvia did not succeed in achieving these objectives. Clinicians and healthcare service providers were not interested in data entry, as they did not see the additional value of these activities but rather an administrative burden. Data entry in the registry was done manually because there were no solutions for data exchange between the Hospital information system (HIS) and the registry. Additionally, the coding standards were outdated. Typically, the data in the existing registry were entered by a medical statistician when all the necessary documentation was provided, and the specific treatment phase was closed. There were also technical problems—at moments when the system was not available. This led to unfavorable results—clinicians were not using it because it meant in practice entering data in an additional siloes system that was not connected to HIS. The data were entered belatedly, were of poor quality, and did not cover all cases. Consequently, the data available in the cancer registry were used only by the CDPC to fulfill their functions, such as providing official statistics and reporting to international organizations. The governance and ownership issue of managing the whole cancer data processing was challenging as the roles of each institution were implemented according to their functions, not taking a holistic perspective on the issue. The recent plan to establish cancer methodological centers and move toward cancer center accreditation is the step taken to strengthen the holistic perspective and determine more clearly the roles of the involved institutions, including data governance.

Initial efforts to improve the existing cancer registry were outlined as early as 2017, immediately after the approval of the new datasets in 2016, with the approval of the political document "Plan for the Improvement of Healthcare Services in the Field of Oncology for 2017-2020." This plan served as the basis for significant advancements in cancer care, and one of its expressed aims was to establish a comprehensive data platform by the end of 2020. The objectives for developing the platform were to facilitate interoperability among various registries and data sources, enabling seamless exchange of information on cancer patient cases. Furthermore, it aimed to incorporate additional datasets crucial for assessing the quality of treatments and evaluating patient outcomes [18].

Regrettably, in 6 years, there have been sporadic and non-consistent efforts and activities, resulting in the development of the new PBCR. Once not having a central EHR system, institutions change to develop individual/silos solutions that served the needs of the individual institution. One of the main obstacles related to the cancer registry was the diverse digital maturity—processes and related data in many medical institutions are either paper-based and not digitized, or not digitized sufficiently. Therefore, the task of developing the new cancer registry was deferred to the subsequent planning period. The funding was not sufficient and was mainly based on EU-financed projects as nationwide it has been the backbone for the digital transformation of all the sectors. As documented in the "Plan for the Improvement of Healthcare Services in the Field of Oncology for 2022-2024," [19] the main issues identified with the existing processes were four as follows: First: Data on the diagnosis and treatment of oncological diseases are incomplete and fragmented, and they do not contain detailed clinical information about the patient. Therefore, it is necessary to improve the registration of oncological disease cases, including both technical solutions and data quality monitoring. The second is that oncological patient data are not readily available and are fragmented. Doctors do not have access to all patient health data related to cancer diagnostics or treatment, leaving patients responsible for "carrying around" their data. The third: There is no way to evaluate the result of therapy, the course of disease development, or the cost and effectiveness of treatment. Fourth: The registration of data on the incidence of cancer cases is based on outdated and insufficiently descriptive classifications for oncology cases and does not provide registration according to European standards in oncology.

Digital transformation and implementation of the new PBCR is not just an IT project but involves changes in process management, as well as changes in regulation, duties and objectives. To deal with the above-mentioned problems, the Plan foreseen two-courses of action: the first—creation of a methodological management center for oncology (with the deadline—the second part of 2024), and the second—development and implementation of the cancer registry and its functionalities (with the starting point in 2022).

Another significant step toward the development of the new cancer registry was participation of Latvia in the OECI project "ICCCS (Latvia DG reform): Improving cancer care coordination and screening in Latvia and Slovakia" [20]. Within the scope of this project several activities were planned: building capacity for population-based cancer registration, improving information systems and assisting oncology centers in receiving accreditation from the Organization of European Cancer Institute [21]. The expertise of the project was divided into three areas: the introduction of effective PBCR, improvements in cancer screening, and the establishment of the Comprehensive Cancer Center and Comprehensive Cancer Network. Overall, it fostered awareness of the needs of oncology, not setting apart the data sets, but designing along the pathway and envisaging the data flows for the purposes of service provision (treatment). It has given also the opportunity to analyze and realize the administrative burden (a process still ongoing), revealing also the silos approach not just regarding the data sets but cooperation as well that hinders the search for better treatment options for patients at a larger scale. And it finally brought different institutions as stakeholders to work together and create together solutions for better cancer patient treatment based on the available data.

As was mentioned in one of the project meetings, the new PBCR will provide the possibility to calculate and analyze the burden of cancer and will help in making decisions for disease control—"to set priorities, resource allocation and evaluate the progress of cancer patient care." As it was pointed out, to allow obtaining indicators that are comparable at the international level—international and up-to-date standards must be followed, as well as "an essential prerequisite for a well-functioning cancer registry is the full involvement of medical institutions and professionals who need to enter these data, ensuring full data entry" [22].

4. Implementation process and influencing factors

Armed with the results and recommendations of previous research on the needs and expectations of the national stakeholders for the New Cancer Registry, as well as the support from the experts of the International Agency of Cancer Research (IARC), the working group for the New Cancer Registry was established in March 2022 with the main responsible institution (see **Figure 1**). According to PBCR development

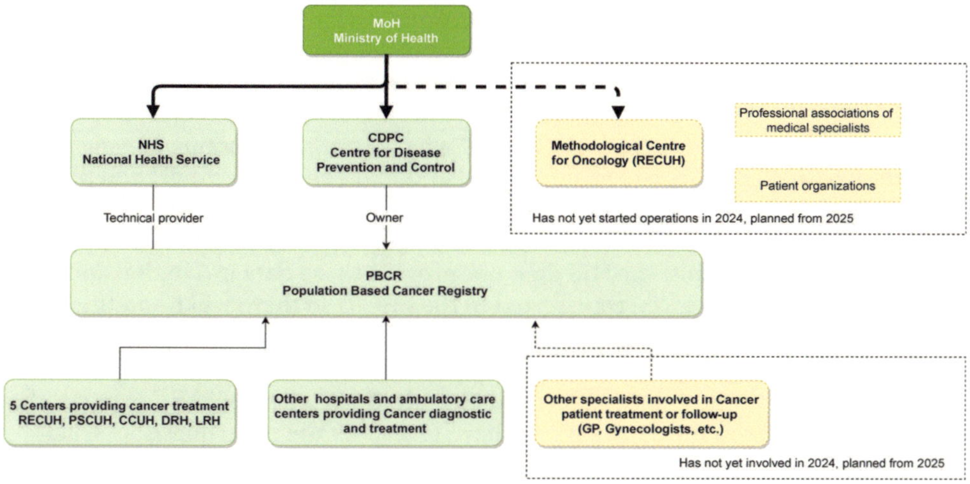

Figure 1.
Main stakeholders in the development of PBCR.

guidelines, provided by IARC, all the recommended elements were considered: required personnel, the physical location of the registry, financing, legal aspects, as well as political will and support, and key stakeholder involvement [23].

The main role in providing political will and legal support, as well as the obligation to establish an advisory committee with the responsibility to oversee the activities in developing the new registry, was granted to the MoH. As the owner of the registry, CPDC was appointed because they were historically responsible for checking the quality of data in the cancer registry, as well as transferring data to international organizations and creating national statistics on the prevalence of cancer in Latvia. As the technical provider for the new registry, NHS was assigned, as they are the responsible authority of the national EHR system. The NHS was also providing technical maintenance and support for the old registry. The responsible body to collaborate with the clinicians and pathologists—RECUH was appointed, as the RECUH is the largest hospital that provides services to Cancer patients, and in the future would become the methodology center for oncology, with the aim to become a comprehensive cancer center. As the main data providers for PBCR, and also users of the information provided by the patient in PBCR, in cases when patients changed institutions where cancer treatment services were received. Cancer patient treatment is provided by five main hospitals: RECUH, Pauls Stradins Clinical University Hospital (PSCUH), Children's Clinical University Hospital (CCUH), as well as Oncology centers in regions: Daugavpils Regional Hospital (DRH) and Liepaja Regional hospital (DRS). Although other healthcare institutions, as well as General Practitioners and specialists, like gynecologists, are involved in Cancer patient diagnostic and follow-up processes, they were not involved in the development of PBCR. Very little, one can say even no involvement, was provided by patient organizations and professional organizations of specialists. This was done deliberately since the expectations of these target groups far exceeded the requirements that were planned to be realized in PBCR. The time frame for PBCR was also taken into account and required a focused approach.

The first round of activities for identifying the needs for the PBCR was led by the RECUH, by carrying out innumerable working groups to identify the needs of the registry with different specialists. Those activities led to unclear and confusing results, as from the one side—the specialists desired to have as much data as possible, to support their needs and interest for improved patient treatment, but also for research needs and treatment outcome analyses. From the other perspective, those clinicians—and experts could not define the necessary data sets to meet their expectations, and usually came to the point: "why we are constructing bicycle, let's take some existing good registry from abroad and make the local copy!" and by mentioning the sample, usually those were clinical registries for the specific kind of cancer. In addition to this, all clinicians in different groups came to the same problem statement—at the moment, the HIS does not provide those data in a digital and structured format, that can be transferred to the PBCR, so there will be additional effort necessary to enter data manually and no one was willing to accept this kind of administrative burden.

After several rounds of discussions and consultations with the IARC experts, the working group came to the decision—we have to answer the main question: what kind of registry we are developing? Hospital-based cancer registry, pathology-based cancer registry or PBCR? As known from the literature, the roles of those registries are different and complementary. The clinical or Hospital-based cancer registry and pathology-based cancer registry—both serve important administrative and clinical functions, but only PBCR can provide "an unbiased profile of the present cancer burden and how it changes over time" [23]. The IARC expert consultations were essential for the focus of further elaboration of the specific registry and also clarify the possible benefits when building PBCR. Since cancer patient data availability and interchangeability were expected by all the involved participants, the pressure and interest in the PBCR elaboration process were high.

There were no necessary data available in the HIS for the clinically expressed needs, and most part of the data needed for the research and treatment outcomes were only available in individual patient paper cards (folders) or not available at all. Therefore, the decision was made that the project would be split into two phases. The first—is the elaboration of the PBCR, according to the contemporary technical and semantical standards, used for the data gathering and analysis for cancer patients. The second phase—is the development of a clinical cancer registry (known as Hospital-based cancer registry), that will be implemented when the HIS, used in the hospitals providing cancer patient care, is changed or upgraded to provide the necessary data in a structured form. Although the decision was to focus and ensure PBCR needs, nevertheless the trade-off was made, that if there are possibilities to provide some additional needs for clinicians by adding some data fields, those additional changes will be implemented. Thereby trying to retain the interest to enter and use data, not only from the CDPD and NHS, but also from the clinician's perspective.

As the scope of the project from "One solution that fits all" was transferred to the relatively narrow scope of the PBCR, and data set with only some additional fields, if there is interest and readiness to enter those data from a practitioner (pathologist, oncologist, chemotherapist and other specialist who treat and manage oncology patients), the main stakeholder for the project and the leader became CDPC. Referring to the literature on how to perform a successful digital transformation (DT) in healthcare, it can be observed, that the case observed was not very successive in proving the multi-stakeholder perspective, as Kraus et al. point out, it is: "critical to understanding properly how in practice, the various players of a healthcare ecosystem (patients, pharmaceutical companies, hospitals, public agencies, and many more) exploit DT technologies and means to quality of care, value creation, and many more managerial issues" [4]. Another author team, led by Ricciardi, notice, that the results and outcomes of DT will "importantly depend on the quality of the process and the involved stakeholders" [24].

With the change of the leading stakeholder, the first objective became the development of the requirements and data set to provide all the necessary information for statistics on national and international levels. So, the first data set was based on the European Network of Cancer Registries Guidelines for the European Cancer Information System (ECIS) [25]. The first data set contained all mandatory fields, that should be collected for the reporting to ECIS.

After the first draft of the new data set was designed, and taking into account the recommendations of the contemporary literature on the subject, the analysis of possibilities to use EHR was performed. Unfortunately, analysis led to results, that with an existing EHR system in Latvia, it is impossible to achieve one of the main aspects covered in Navijou et al., point out that "the objective of each patient registry will be achieved if the registered data are reliable," by this focusing on accuracy, completeness, and timeliness, especially in the circumstances when data are submitted to "impartial, independent quality control process" [26].

Analysis of the data necessary for the ECIS data set indicated that there is no information about the diagnoses available at required semantical standards. An in-depth analysis of the Latvian case led to the same findings as in Post et al. research: "Inadequate data exchange between providers is largely due to inadequate EHR data standardization. Most EHR implementations have site-specific codes that are ill documented" [27]. As mentioned by Gosh et al.: "Effective standards for data interchange help break down silos in the healthcare systems" [28]. As the existing national EHR system was used mostly as an accounting system, except for two modules: E-prescriptions and Sick-ness leave certificates, the available clinical information was very minimal. Therefore, the only information about the person that can be used from the national EHR system—is the demographic characteristics of the patient. Therefore, to provide necessary data for PBCR, one of the requirements was to develop a data entry form, where clinicians or medical statisticians enter the data necessary for the PBCR (or enter data in local HIS and send to the PBCR system using API, when the necessary changes will be implemented in HIS).

The next significant decision was to decide on the scope of the cases for which the data should be entered. After several discussions, the decision was made that the scope will be according to the ECIS guidelines about the diagnoses that will be included, and reporting cases—which means all cases that are diagnosed in Latvia. In addition, to provide local needs for analyzing the provided services to Cancer patients in Latvia—to broaden the scope and provide information on all cases, no matter where the diagnostic was performed and who is paying for the diagnostic or treatment services: state-paid, private insurance or out-of-pocket. The decision to provide a wider scope was related to the existing practice, related to person mobility and the war in Ukraine when hospitals in Latvia provided further diagnostic and treatment services for foreign patients and refugees. By adding the additional field "country of diagnostic," the registry could satisfy two requirements at the same time: for reporting to international registries and serving as PBCR—including only the cases diagnosed in Latvia. However, to analyze the number of Cancer patients in Latvia and evaluate the need for services and other related information, can use information of all patients who have received Cancer treatment-related services in Latvia, no matter where the cancer was diagnosed.

The next sequential process was to validate and verify data sets with the clinicians, as they are the main source of information necessary for the PBCR. During these activities, the main findings were related to the mapping issues—mapping existing classifiers that were used in existing cancer registries and the data needed for reporting to ECIS. That led to some amendments in the existing classifiers, adding new classifiers and data fields, as well as a total change of values used in existing cancer registry classifiers. The most significant changes were related to the change of the version used for disease coding, from ICD-O-2 to ICD-O-3.2, and from TNM 7th to TNM 8th version.

The following task was to analyze and provide additional information that is necessary for the clinicians or other parties, has been collected previously, but is not a part of ECIS. During this activity, there were data fields that were removed—as the analysis of the existing data showed, those data fields usually are not filled and as the fill-out range is very small, are not used for the analysis. Other changes were related to the outdated coding systems. Some classifications were kept unchanged from the previous version: for example, ORPHA codes for rare disease cancer cases. A significant change was implemented for the pediatric field, as the existing registry and ECIS data fields did not provide the necessary data for the pediatricians. Based on the Finnish experience [29], CCUH insisted on the implementation of ICCC-3 (International Classification of Childhood Cancer version 3).

Information about received treatment and the course of the disease, according to ECIS, contains only information about the type of treatment the patient received. As the previous cancer registry contained more data fields, a decision was made that all the data fields that existed in the old registry would be entered also into the new registry. Objectives of this decision were grounded in the will to analyze the outcomes of the patient treated with one or another therapy. During this phase, some additional fields were added—for example, therapy line, the type of the therapy, information about termination and related reasons, etc. Demand from clinicians for adding fields characterizing the treatment was much higher, as the data fields were approved for inclusion in the registry. Currently there is no possibility to enter this information in HIS, which healthcare institutions use, and the risk that data would not be entered is too high. Considering this, the implementation of these additional needs was postponed to the next phase, when HIS would provide this information in an electronically available format.

Another desired aspect was related to providing information about the different diagnostic tests performed on cancer patients related to molecular and cytogenetic examination and results. In those data sets were interested clinicians as well as NHS, pharmacy, and also patient NGOs. This interest was related to the treatment possibilities and state-paid medication, which is provided for the patients with specific clinical findings. Of course, this is not in the scope of classical PBCR, but as it is related to state-paid services for cancer patients, the motivation for such data inclusion is clear. However, its implementation was added to the "waiting list" until there would be structured data on laboratory and genomic testing findings.

The next phase, which followed data set development, was the technical implementation of the new registry. Technically PBCR became a part of the national E-health ecosystem, thus providing possibilities for the medical professionals working with cancer patients, to get safe and appropriate access to the data in PBCR and through PBCR share data on Cancer patients, who are involved in the treatment of the patient. Providing and sharing data among the medical practitioners who provide services to the patient, is not a usual function of PBCR, but in Latvia's case, PBCR carries out a function, that should be provided classically by EHR. In these circumstances, it is the fundamental benefit and "carrot" for the medical professionals to enter the data of the Cancer patients in PBCR. Of course, at the time, when there will be fully implemented and used EHR providing all the data about Cancer patient diagnostics and treatment electronically in structured and standardized data format, PBCR will give away the role of providing data to clinicians.

While developing the PBCR, local systems used in healthcare facilities did not provide the necessary data for the PBCR and at the beginning all the data had to be entered manually, using the PBCR system data entry forms. But, looking forward, normally those systems also should be adjusted to collect all the necessary data and provide the possibility for medical practitioners to enter data only once—in the development of PBCR one of the principles was "API first" (Application programming interface—which provide interoperability possibilities to exchange data from system to system). So, the API services were designed to ensure that when HIS would be adjusted to provide entrance of the necessary data in those local systems practitioners' daily work—all the necessary data would be submitted automatically from HIS to PBCR. In case when Cancer patient comes to visit the doctor, the HIS will request data from PBCR and demonstrate all the available information from PBCR into the system doctor uses.

The implementation process of the PBCR was executed in three directions: (1) technical implementation of the ICT system, (2) changes in legal acts and (3) activities related to the introduction of the new data standard and data set. The communication about the PBCR was not indicated as a priority, at the same time it would have managed the expectations of different stakeholders better if it had been provided regularly on the elaboration process and expected practical outcomes. Technical implementation started when the first data set was approved and the content of the necessary data sets and classifiers approved with the industry. To provide the possibility for both: the NHS system as well as HIS to start implementation of new data sets, the first technical task was to provide all new classifiers in the national EHR system. The following process was the implementation of HL7 FHIR profiles and API services to provide the possibility to submit data to PBCR in the system-system approach in accordance with the principle "API first." The following task was to develop data entry forms in the scope of the existing national EHR system to provide the possibility for those medical practitioners whose HIS does not provide the possibility to submit data automatically, to enter the data directly in the PBCR system. The next task was acceptance testing made by the CDPC experts and some pilot practitioners. During this phase, the need for adding extra controls and checks arise, to improve the quality and completeness of the entered data. At this moment, technically the new PBCR was ready for piloting.

The next step was related to transferring data from the old registry to the new PBCR. As the patient is diagnosed once but receives treatment and follow-up for several years, to avoid the necessity to enter old data into the new registry, the decision was made to transfer all the cancer patient disease cards from the old registry to the new PBCR. As the old registry used other data standards (old versions and additional fields, that were not implemented in the new registry) the next challenge was how to transfer that data. Analysis showed that the best way would be to transfer the data as they are, not even trying to convert old data to new standards. As a result, there were additional fields added to the data entry forms. For the user, that means that data fields and used classifiers in fields changed depending on the diagnosis date for the disease card and depending on the treatment start date for the treatment card.

During the first conversation process, due to data quality control, a significant proportion of the data from the old system was not transferred to the new registry.

As the aim was to convert as much as possible data from the old registry to the new registry, quality controls of the old data were optimized to a minimal level and some automatic corrective activities with the incoherent data were done. It took significant additional work from the IT development part—to provide all the additional classifiers and different controls used in the old system to use in the new system, but it paid off, as the clinicians and CDPC were pleased that all data are available in one system.

The other part of the activities was related to the change in regulations related to the PBCR. It involved changes in the Patients' Rights Law and several Cabinet of Ministers Regulations. Despite the identified amendments to those legal acts at the start of the project in the first part of 2022, it took much more time than it was envisaged for the necessary changes. Due to the long negotiating process on the regulation, the new standard and data set, that was planned to become active since July 1, 2023, was postponed to January 1, 2024.

The third and even one of the most significant parts of the project implementation was to assess and provide readiness for the industry to use the new semantic standards and data sets. This task was assigned to CDPC and RECUH. One of the time-consuming parts was the introduction of the ICD-O-3.2 instead of the previously used ICD-O-2, done by the CDPC. This activity contained an official translation of the ICD-O-3.2 classification in Latvian, as well as review and updates in methodological materials about appropriate cancer case coding, as well as several educational activities providing on-site and online and providing all related information on CDPC and NHS online sites for medical professionals.

Although all those activities were performed before the regulation became active, and there was the assumption that all the parties would be ready for data entrance and further processing—unfortunately, it raised more and more questions from the clinicians and pathologists about the appropriate coding and data entry. Just as the experience of the world on DT in the healthcare sector shows problems arise when there are changes in organizational workflows. As described by Iyanna et al. research indicated "linked resistance among doctors and clinical staff to these stakeholders concerns regarding changes in workflows and organizational issues," and other influencing factors indicated by the authors are "additional time these professionals may be required to integrate these innovations into their practice." Authors also pointed out, that another key organizational obstacle for successive change implementation is related to "lack of training and routines, deficient IT support, and lack of infrastructure" [30]. All those problems were observed on the hospital side, during the development and implementation of the PBCR.

5. Conclusion

During the new cancer registry development and implementation process there were a lot of tangled puns, moments of lowering the hands, discouragement, as well as some real inspirational and empowering moments. However, the main lessons learned are summarized in the following TOP five conclusions.

First: To achieve the result—there should be a clear understanding from all the parties that are involved, and what goals we want to achieve. Furthermore, commitment is necessary to keep the focus, and not to lose time by desiring new assets and delaying development. As the presented experience showed, a lot of time was spent on discussions about what kind or registry we are designing, who would be the main stakeholders and what are the goals of our project. At the same time, the co-designing experience in Latvia is new, and adjustments to it are necessary in all sectors, not exclusively healthcare. Overall, we can be satisfied with the achieved results, as the developed registry provides all the necessary tasks, that PBCR should provide and in advance, there is additional information that can be used for quality and treatment outcome analyze and also can be used for service planning purposes. But the question remains—should this be provided in the PBCR or EHR system?

Second: To promote progress—appropriate stakeholders, defined roles and tasks must be determined. Our experience showed that we could have possibly escaped some needless working groups and discussions if the main stakeholders had been appointed for the specific purpose at the beginning. A significant proportion of discussions with clinicians and patient NGOs resulted in quite a long wish list that was not implemented in the scope of the PBCR. On one side—it is good to have all these needs, that we could work on in the future, but on the other side—those stakeholders were disappointed that they participated in meetings and devoted their precious time, but most of the needs were not implemented. But those problems were directly related to the first challenge: we did not know at the beginning what we would develop as the wish was "one that fits all!" and as little administrative burden as possible.

Third: To become successful implementers—there is a need for change promoters in all related levels: political, methodological and in industry. We were privileged as we had those change promoters at all levels: there were individuals who were change promoters and came from the Ministry of Health, CDPC, NHS and also some clinicians and pathologists who believed in the idea of the new cancer registry. Besides those directly involved stakeholders—there was support also from the other directly not involved parties: pharmacy NGOs, the committee in Parliament, the state president chancellery, academia and AmCham. During the implementation phase, the main and most effective change promoter was representative of CDPC who at the same time was a practicing oncologist—chemotherapist with an excellent reputation among medical professionals, thus strengthening the support for the new registry among clinicians.

Fourth: To move fast toward the goals—there is a need for effective decision-making and competency. As our experience revealed—it is good to rely on international standards and guidelines, as well as to have the possibility to consult experts, but that does not guarantee that those obtained knowledge will provide the ideal model of the registry. Our case showed, the influencing hindering factor in Latvia case was the absence of effective EHR system, which provides all the information on the medical services patient receive. So, we could not use the experience from the literature to use EHR, but to satisfy the needs for our clinicians and medical statisticians, we significantly broadened the scope of classical PBCR. To design the appropriate model—there is a need for the decision-makers—who are ready to work in circumstances of uncertainty and ready to take risks.

Fifth: Developing new registry—is not an ICT project, but digital transformation process! Therefore, the main success factors rely on the cooperation and collaboration of all involved parties from health policy creators, through health service providers and supervisors, to medical practitioners and patients. The available data sets allow us to draw conclusions and come up with solutions for the changes in service provision. Moreover, the components of success are: a good mix of competencies, dedicated leadership and great project management skills, but excellent results are not imaginable without change promoters who believe in the success and benefits of this project, and keep it moving especially in times of tough decisions when financial and timing resources are scarce. Clear communication on the work done is also essential and, in our case, (as mentioned above) still more could have been done if this aspect had been more emphasized.

Authors identify that further research is necessary to enhance the understanding of data governance in digital transformation process as it has been one of the problematic issues to insure faster DT in healthcare. Without it, digital health ecosystems may not sufficiently respond to the challenging and growing needs and priorities of health systems, not ensuring transparency and dynamic development. It has been assumed that strong governance determines the roles and responsibilities of each involved party very explicitly, including the provision of the necessary resources.

Author details

Aiga Balode and Ieva Bikava*
Riga Stradins University, Riga, Latvia

*Address all correspondence to: ieva.bikava@rsu.lv

References

[1] Vial G. Understanding digital transformation: A review and a research agenda. The Journal of Strategic Information Systems. 2019;**28**(2):118-144. DOI: 10.1016/j.jsis.2019.01.003

[2] World Economic Forum. Transforming Healthcare: Navigating Digital Health with a Value-Driven Approach. Insight Report. 2024. p. 3. Available from: https://www.weforum.org/publications/transforming-healthcare-navigating-digital-health-with-a-value-driven-approach/ [Accessed: September 11, 2024]

[3] Marcelo A et al. Transforming Health Systems Through Good Digital Governance, ADB Sustainable Development Working Paper Series. No.51. Philippines: Asian Development Bank; 2018. Available from: https://www.adb.org/publications/transforming-health-systems-good-digital-health-governance [Accessed: September 11, 2024]

[4] Kraus S et al. Digital transformation in healthcare: Analyzing the current state-of-research. Journal of Business Research. 2021;**123**:557-567. DOI: 10.1016/j.jbusres.2020.10.030

[5] OECD. Beating Cancer Inequalities in the EU. Spotlight on Cancer Prevention and Early Detection. OECD Health Policy Studies. Available from: https://health.ec.europa.eu/publications/beating-cancer-inequalities-eu-spotlight-cancer-prevention-and-early-detection_en [Accessed: September 11, 2024]

[6] Pop B et al. The role of medical registries, potential applications and limitations. Epidemiology. Medicine and Pharmacy Reports. 2019;**92**(1):7-14. DOI: 10.15386/cjmed-1015

[7] White MC et al. The history and use of cancer registry data by public health cancer control programs in the United States. Cancer. 2017;**123**(Suppl/24):4969-4976. DOI: 10.1002/cncr.30905

[8] Tucker TC et al. Unlocking the potential of population-based cancer registries. Cancer. 1 Nov 2019;**125**(21):3729-3737. DOI: 10.1002/cncr.32355

[9] Nicholas N, Perego A. Interoperability of population-based patient registries. Journal of Biomedical Informatics: X. Sep 2020;**6**:100074. DOI: 10.1016/j.yjbinx.2020.100074

[10] Garmann-Johnsen NF et al. Employee-driven digitalization in healthcare: Codesigning services that deliver. Health Policy and Technology. 2020;**9**(2):247-254. DOI: 10.1016/j.hlpt.2020.03.001

[11] Health Level Seven International. Home Page. Available from: www.hl7.org [Accessed: September 11, 2024]

[12] Posadas-Martinez MM et al. The role of registries in improving health and bridging healthcare, research, education, innovation and development: A research department perspective. Journal of International Medical Research. 2024;**52**(3):1-13. DOI: 10.1177/03000605241233|40

[13] Mery L, Bray F. Population-based cancer registries: A gateway to improved surveillance of non-communicable diseases. Ecancermedicalscience. 2020;**14**:ed95. DOI: 10.3332/ecancer.2020.ed95

[14] Thong MSY et al. Population-based cancer registries for quality-of-life

research. A work-in-progress resource for survivorship studies? Cancer. 1 Jun 2013;**119**(Suppl 11):2109-2123. DOI: 10.1002/cncr.28056

[15] Thompson CA et al. Population-based registry linkages to improve validity of electronic health record-based cancer research. Cancer Epidemiology, Biomarkers & Prevention. 2020;**29**:796-806. DOI: 10.1158/1055-9965.EPI-19-0882

[16] Health Statistics DataBase of Latvia. Data Set: IRS10. Population at the Beginning of Year, Population Change and Key Vital Statistics. Population at Beginning of Year. 2024. Available from: https://data.stat.gov.lv/pxweb/en/OSP_PUB/START__POP__IR__IRS/IRS010/ [Accessed: September 11, 2024]

[17] Cabinet of Ministers of Latvia. Regulation nr.748: Amendments to Cabinet Regulation No. 134 of 11 March 2014 "Regulations Regarding the Unified Electronic Information System of the Health Sector". Entry Into Force: 01.12.2016. Available from: https://likumi.lv/ta/id/286939 [Accessed: September 11, 2024]

[18] Cabinet of Ministers of Latvia. Policy Document. Plan for the Improvement of Healthcare Services in the Field of Oncology 2017-2020. Available from: https://likumi.lv/ta/id/291187-par-veselibas-aprupes-pakalpojumu-onkologijas-joma-uzlabosanas-planu-2017-2020-gadam [Accessed: September 11, 2024]

[19] Cabinet of Ministers of Latvia. Policy Document. Plan for the Improvement of Healthcare Services in the field of Oncology 2022-2024. Available from: https://likumi.lv/ta/id/333775-par-veselibas-aprupes-pakalpojumu-uzlabosanas-planu-onkologijas-joma-2022-2024-gadam [Accessed: September 11, 2024]

[20] OECI. OECI Project Overview. Project Details. ICCCS (Latvia DG Reforms). Available from: https://oeci.eu/ProjectDetails.aspx?id=7 [Accessed: September 11, 2024]

[21] International Agency for Research on Cancer. Media Center. IARC Launches the Improving Cancer Care Coordination and Screening in Latvia and Slovakia (ICCCS) Project. 2022. Available from: https://www.iarc.who.int/news-events/icccs_project/ [Accessed: September 11, 2024]

[22] The Baltic Times. Changes are Expected in the Care of Care Patients in Latvia. 2023. Available from: https://www.baltictimes.com/changes_are_expected_in_the_care_of_cancer_patients_in_latvia/ [Accessed: September 11, 2024]

[23] International Agency for Research on Cancer. IARC Technical Report No. 43. Planning and Developing Population-Based Cancer Registration in Low- or Middle-Income Countries. 2014. Available from: https://www.ncbi.nlm.nih.gov/books/NBK566957/ [Accessed: September 11, 2024]

[24] Ricciardi W et al. European Journal of Public Health; **29**(Suppl. 3):7-12. DOI: 10.1093/eurpub/ckz165

[25] European Network of Cancer Registries. Call for Data Protocol for European Population-Based Cancer Registries. 2022. Available from: https://encr.eu/sites/default/files/Data_call/ECIS%20call%20for%20data%20protocol_20240226.pdf [Accessed: September 11, 2024]

[26] Nahvijou A et al. Using electronic health record system to establish a national patients registry: Lessons learned from the cancer registry in Iran. International Journal of Medical

Informatics. Dec 2023;**180**:105245. DOI: 10.1016/j.ijmedinf.2023.105245

[27] Post AR, Burningham Z, Halwani AS. Electronic health record data in cancer learning health systems: Challenges and opportunities. JCO Clinical Cancer Informatics. Mar 2022;**6**:e2100158. DOI: 10.1200/CCI.21.00158

[28] Ghosh K et al. Digital transformation in healthcare: Insights on value creation. Journal of Computer Information Systems. 2022;**63**(2):449-459. DOI: 10.1080/088774417.2022.2070798

[29] Jokela M, Leinonen MK, Malila N, Taskinen M, Madanat-Harjuoja. Completeness of pediatric cancer registration in the Finnish Cancer Registry. Acta Oncologica. Nov 2019;**58**(11):1577-1580. DOI: 10.1080/0284186X.2019.1638522

[30] Iyanna S et al. Digital transformation of healthcare sector. What is impeding adoption and continued usage of technology-driven innovations by end-users? Journal of Business Research. 2022;**153**:150-161. DOI: 10.1016/j.jbusres.2022.08.007

Chapter 8

ICT Competencies and Citizen Participation in Students of a Public University in Peru – 2024

Jaime Rodrigo and Salazar Espinoza

Abstract

Digital citizenship, or citizen participation, is defined as the ability of citizens to participate in society in an informed and responsible manner through digital technologies. The objective of this original empirical research is to determine how ICT skills are related to citizen participation in students of a public university in Peru in the year 2024. For this purpose, a self-assessment of their ICT skills and their performance in control activities in local management will be carried out. A non-experimental cross-sectional design was used, obtaining a convenience sample of students from the Faculty of Business Sciences of the National University of Huancavelica, Peru, in the year 2024. The techniques and instruments for data collection and analysis were structured questionnaires for face-to-face surveys. The results showed contradictory findings: students excel in the use of ICTs, but there is little citizen participation in public affairs. It is urgent to develop government policies that encourage digital citizen participation in the country, improving the implementation of digital channels, both external and internal, by municipalities. This will contribute to a digital government process that encourages greater citizen participation and the digitization of its services.

Keywords: ICT competencies, digital citizenship, citizen participation, digital government, transparency

1. Introduction

Today, Information and Communication Technologies (ICT) are essential to optimize citizen participation in the management of public services at the local level. There is a clear relationship between ICT Competencies and actively empowering citizens to get involved in public affairs. This connection enables people to become active participants in decisions made by authorities that affect their community.

ICT skills refer to the abilities required to use digital tools effectively. These skills help citizens access important information, communicate with authorities, and participate in discussions on local issues. On the other hand, digital citizenship does not only imply the use of technology, but also the ability to participate critically and constructively in the digital world, which promotes transparency, access to information and sharing responsibility in public management [1, 2].

By developing ICT Competencies, we foster a more informed and active citizenry, capable of influencing local decisions and the quality of public services. This article analyses how strengthening these skills can improve citizen participation and, in turn, optimize local management, creating a beneficial cycle for both citizens and government institutions.

Civic engagement by university students through digital skills presents clear symptoms of a lack of political and social involvement. In China, a study found that although students have a good level of digital literacy, only 23% actively participate in civic activities online, due to a "weak political concern" [3]. In Saudi Arabia, although 60% of students are comfortable using the Internet, only 20% engage in civic activities online, citing a lack of reliable platforms and a perception of political irrelevance [4].

The problem is attributed to causes such as the influence of a lack of incentives, distrust in institutions, and a perception of political irrelevance in digital platforms [5]. In Russia, students face challenges due to a lack of educational coordination and the need to increase digital skills in educational programs, which affects their civic participation [6]. In Saudi Arabia, although students have good attitudes toward using the Internet, the lack of reliable platforms and the perception of political irrelevance limit their participation [7].

This disconnect can be attributed to factors such as a lack of incentives, distrust in institutions, and the perceived irrelevance of digital platforms for political participation. If these issues are not addressed, the consequence will be a less engaged and participatory citizenry, which will weaken democracies and governance at the global level. To mitigate this problem, it is recommended to improve the integration of digital skills in educational curricula and promote more attractive and trustworthy participation platforms.

In Peru, the problem of civic participation among university students is reflected in the low adoption of digital skills for civic engagement. Although Peruvian students are increasingly familiar with the use of electronic devices and digital platforms, their participation in civic and political processes remains limited. This situation is due to the lack of adequate infrastructure, few digital literacy programs, and distrust of the digital channels offered by local governments [8].

Failure to implement effective and engaging ICT channels for citizen participation risks perpetuating a cycle of civic disinterest and digital exclusion. Failure to address these issues will also result in a less engaged global citizenry, weakening democracies and global governance. These figures reflect a global trend where high digital literacy does not translate into effective civic participation, highlighting the need to improve digital platforms and incentives for political participation among young people. However, possible solutions include investing in technological infrastructure, promoting educational programs focused on digital skills, and strengthening transparency and trust in e-participation systems.

The use of ICTs has proven to be effective in increasing citizen participation. Tools such as the globally used CONSUL application improve transparency and accountability [9]. Crowdsourcing allows citizens to contribute ideas to solve local problems, encouraging co-production and improving urban services [10]. Tools such as e-ILAUD promote participation in urban design, adapting solutions to community needs [11]. In smart cities such as Jakarta and Kuala Lumpur, ICTs have increased citizen participation and optimized public services [12], and finally, the integration of *"blockchain"* in e-participation systems has increased transparency and security in democratic participation such as the techniques referred to by [13].

In this context, the research asks: *¿How do ICT Competencies and their dimensions relate to citizen participation in students at a public university in the Huancavelica region of Peru?*

Likewise, the objective was to determine the relationship between both variables and the dimensions of ICT Competencies.

2. Theoretical framework

2.1 Previous studies

The international precedents examined in this paper [9, 14, 15] converge in their analysis of e-participation, highlighting the fundamental role played by information and communication technologies (ICT) in facilitating and improving citizen participation in governance processes. Each study underlines the relevance of these digital technologies, whether through e-participation platforms, specific regulations, or tools developed for this purpose, in expanding the capacity of citizens to actively engage in public decision-making. Furthermore, all three studies agree that the adoption of digital participation mechanisms has a considerable impact on governance by promoting greater transparency, accountability, and the possibility of more inclusive and effective governance. They also explain a growing trend toward the digitalization of citizen participation as an instrument to strengthen democratic processes and optimize the interaction between citizens and government institutions.

However, the methodologies employed in the three studies vary depending on their contexts. In Adam and Dzang [14], they use an advanced quantitative approach, combining structural equation modeling (PLS-SEM) with necessary condition analysis (NCA) to explore causal and mediating relationships in a global context. In contrast, in Secinaro et al. [9] they apply a systematic combination approach based on an "abductive" process, which integrates different methodologies to analyze a specific case study and generalize the findings to broader theories. Meanwhile, in Santamaria-Philco et al. [15] they employ the Design Science Research (DSR) methodology together with the SCRUM method to develop and evaluate the effectiveness of a specific technological tool in improving e-participation. The three studies present significant differences in their research approach and context.

There are three other studies carried out [16–18], the first one carried out in Nigeria, the second one in the United States, and the last one resulting from online surveys, they agree in demonstrating a direct causal relationship between ICT Competencies and citizen participation, using surveys as the primary source of information to support their findings, from the use of a deductive method. Finally, we find the study by Cabero-Almenara and Palacios-Rodríguez [19], whose objective was to evaluate how e-government technologies influence voter participation in the US, using a deductive methodology based on surveys of local governments and data analysis with online electoral information indexes, they find findings such as that the use of ICT tools increases electoral participation, showing the direct influence of the skills.

2.2 ICT competencies

2.2.1 Definitions

ICT competence according to the European Framework of Digital Competence for Teachers "DigCompEdu" is defined as the ability to effectively and critically use digital technologies to obtain access, management, integration, evaluation, creation and communication of information. The competences involve knowledge of the processes that ICTs carry out, the skills to technically manage digital tools and the attitudes that are guided by the ethical and responsible use of these tools, whose components will be subject to community monitoring, which has an impact on society [19].

These competencies are also observed to understand the levels of complexity and specialization; therefore, they require in-depth mastery of technological skills with gradual learning that contains criteria of exploring, integrating, and innovating [20].

According to the OECD and UNESCO, ICT Competencies are essential for educational and professional development in the current context. They synthesize the combination of knowledge, skills, and attitudes regarding the use of digital technologies in various contexts. They are basic aspects for students to interact and learn in technological environments as a support for their academic training [21, 22]. The OECD summarizes its contributions as follows: The user navigates in a digital environment using tools to access and evaluate the information available on the Internet; he or she also collaborates and communicates his or her findings and seeks solutions to problems based on his or her ability to use and adapt technologies. This approach alludes to the fact that users should improve their critical and creative capacities [21].

UNESCO [23] has developed the "ICT Competence Framework for Teachers", which is a set of 18 systematized competencies around six key aspects of the teaching professional in his practical life such as: "Understanding the role of ICT in educational policies, Curriculum, and evaluation, Pedagogy, Application of digital competences, Organization and administration and Professional learning of teachers" (p. 9).

2.2.2 Dimensions

"ICT Competencies" as a support, referring to the set of knowledge, skills and attitudes necessary to assertively use digital technologies. They also include the ability to operate technological devices, manage software and applications, search and evaluate content on the Internet [24]*"on line"* or online information, and use these technologies in an ethical and safe manner.

In this scenario [24], the first dimension of the variable "ICT Competencies" is defined as the "knowledge" of theoretical and practical information that students have to use ICT effectively in their daily tasks. This includes knowledge about technological tools and their application in the educational context. Regarding the theories that support it, there are studies by Refs. [25, 26], on "Digital Literacy" or ICT knowledge, whose indicators are; use of electronic devices, software and applications, understanding of digital concepts and terminology and, access and use of digital information whose search deserves a critical evaluation of the quality and reliability of digital information, knowledge about the security and privacy of information.

Likewise, the second dimension, known as "skills" (abilities) [24], is known as the practical capacities that allow students to apply their knowledge in real situations. They imply the ability to use ICT in their daily lives, design learning activities, and solve problems that arise in the educational process. Communication and Digital

Collaboration. According to the theoretical support [27, 28], they propose the measurement of their indicators from the use of social networks and communication platforms for citizen participation, skills to work on online community projects, competence in the creation and management of digital communities. Also, the factors that affect the adoption of e-Participation through social networks at a local level are integrated, which can be measured with indicators from the use of citizen participation platforms, participation in digital social campaigns and movements, interaction with institutions and public organizations, among others.

Finally, in Ref. [24], there is the third dimension: "attitudes", a component that encompasses the application of ethical values, the control of their emotions, interests, and personality traits that influence teaching practice, adapted to the reality of students. Attitudes are crucial for students' willingness to integrate ICTs into their daily lives and continue the process of assimilation to changes in the learning environment. From Refs. [29, 30], the theoretical supports of the "attitudes" dimension are extracted, considering: (a) the critical attitude toward digital information, whose indicators can be measured through the critical and ethical evaluation of digital information, as well as awareness and responsibility regarding the security and privacy of personal and collective information; and (b) digital innovation and creativity, with its indicators: development of digital community projects, use of emerging technologies to involve citizens, promotion of creative practice and critical thinking. I have made adjustments to improve the clarity and fluidity of the text.

In summary, the variable "ICT Competencies" is broken down into three dimensions: knowledge, skills, and attitudes. The first dimension, "knowledge", covers the theoretical and practical information necessary for the effective use of ICTs, including digital literacy and critical evaluation of information [18, 19]. The second dimension, "skills", refers to the practical application of this knowledge in real situations, such as the use of social networks and communication platforms for the practice of digital citizenship by collaborating on online community projects [20, 21]. Finally, the "attitudes" dimension includes the motivation and ethical values to integrate ICTs in daily life, highlighting the critical attitude toward digital information and digital innovation and creativity [22, 23].

2.3 Citizen participation

2.3.1 Definitions

"Citizen Participation" refers to the process in which individuals actively engage in decision-making related to political, social, and community issues. This can include everything from voting in elections to participating in public consultations, online discussion forums, and collaborations with government agencies to influence public policy and administrative decisions [31].

This concept is reinforced by the opinion of the OECD, which has stressed that citizen participation through digital means is crucial for transparency and the enhancement of democracy. Countries with high levels of ICT development and democracy, such as OECD member nations, are more likely to achieve a high level of digital social innovation. This reinforces the relationship between the development of ICT Competencies and the practice of citizenship, emphasizing the need to integrate these skills into educational systems to strengthen democracy [32].

There are other definitions that accompany the concepts of sustainability and governance, and the challenges and proposals that citizen participation deserves.

Regarding the first, e-participation is essential for sustainable development, since it improves the relationship between citizens and public institutions. ICTs provide tools that allow greater participation in decision-making, which is an essential task for inclusive governance [29] and the second, referring to the advantages of digital citizen participation, its implementation faces significant challenges, such as the lack of trust in digital platforms and the disconnection between citizens and governments. The lack of incentives and the perception of political irrelevance also hinder the adoption of these technologies [33].

In short, citizen participation implies active involvement in political, social, and community decisions, using means such as voting, public consultations, and digital platforms. The integration of ICT Competencies is important to strengthen democracy and inclusive governance, not only in developed countries but also where democracy, institutions, and public management are weak. However, challenges such as distrust in digital platforms and the perception of political irrelevance hinder the effective implementation of e-participation, which is essential for sustainable development and the relationship between citizens and public institutions.

The task of local government remains to provide digital channels, platforms for access to information on the Internet, make its management transparent, and seek governance between authorities and the community in order to legitimize its actions, among other issues. This reflection also leads to a survey of the concepts that [34] examine the concepts of governance proposed by the OECD, highlighting its role as one of the main entities in global governance that promotes standards of efficiency, transparency, and responsibility in public and corporate administration at a global level.

2.3.2 Dimensions

Article 31 of the 1993 Peruvian Political Constitution guarantees citizen participation as a fundamental action. It clearly establishes the rights of citizens in relation to their involvement in public affairs. This article guarantees that citizens have the right to participate in electoral processes, referendums, legislative initiatives, and the removal or revocation of authorities, as well as to demand accountability [35]. The importance of this article lies in the fact that it not only recognizes the rights of citizens to be elected and to elect their representatives but also establishes active participation as a civic duty. In addition, it promotes mechanisms of direct and indirect participation in municipal government, which strengthens democracy and governance in the country.

Likewise, there is Law No. 26300, known as the Law on the Rights of Participation and Citizen Control in Peru, which establishes a legal framework that regulates citizen participation in public management [36]. This law includes various mechanisms that allow citizens to get involved in political, social, and civic processes. On the other hand, Law 27,972, or the Organic Law of Municipalities, emphasizes the importance of citizen participation in public affairs through their municipalities [37]. Both guarantees, institutionalize and encourage neighborhood participation in decision-making in local management, and are essential to strengthening democracy in Peru because it promotes the active participation of citizens in decision-making that affects their lives.

By establishing a set of mechanisms for political, social, and civic participation, the norms aim to promote a more transparent and responsible government, in which the voice of citizens is heard and taken into account in public management. These mechanisms served as a theoretical support or basis for defining the dimensions of citizen participation, the processes of which must be implemented in local governments throughout the country.

On the one hand, we have "political participation" as the first dimension, in this part the following indicators were considered: "electoral participation" where the citizen actively participates in general, regional and municipal elections to elect their authorities, elects and is elected as a representative of local coordination organizations to support management; the "Constitutional Reform Initiative" that empowers citizens to present constitutional reform projects, which must be supported by a number of signatures equivalent to 0.3% of the electorate; the "Legislative Initiative" where citizens can propose bills to Congress, whose analysis is guided by the cost-benefit and the impact of the norm; likewise, there is the "Referendum" initiative where citizens can participate in popular consultation processes to approve or reject laws, regional norms or municipal ordinances; likewise, there is the "Removal of Authorities" that allows citizens to demand the removal of authorities for failure to perform their duties; and finally the "Ordinance Initiative" which is a mechanism with regional and local characteristics allowing citizens to propose ordinances that regulate specific aspects of their communities.

On the other hand, there is the second dimension, "social participation", which the law provides for participation mechanisms considered as indicators for the study: "Participatory Budgets" where the involvement of citizens in the planning and execution processes of municipal budgets is contemplated, whose decisions allow the allocation of resources in local projects in an efficient manner; in "Accountability" citizens demand accountability from the authorities, management transparency in the use of resources and budget execution; and, finally, "Citizen Oversight" which consists of supervision of public management by citizens to ensure that authorities comply with their obligations and act for the benefit of the community.

The study considers that these measures are part of a social rather than a political perspective, as a scenario of citizen surveillance, generation of trust, and strengthening of democracy through social participation. Citizens engage in these acts as a social prerogative because it is understood that they will help the community more than a party or democracy. Unfortunately, in Peru, institutions are still quite weak, and poor management practices by the authorities would incur social and economic costs.

Finally, the variable presents the third dimension, "civic participation," where we find various channels of local participation. Citizens demonstrate their civic spirit by participating in civic activities because they must join various committees and local coordination organizations to support local management. Here we have: "Open town hall meetings," which are public meetings convened by the local government to discuss matters of general interest, so that citizens can express their opinions and propose solutions to local problems; "management committees," which are neighborhood organizations that work in coordination with municipalities to support the planning and execution of development projects in their communities; "Roundtables," which are spaces for dialog and coordination between the municipality, social organizations, and the general public, whose purpose is to build consensus on local public policies and monitor their implementation.

Civic participation at the local level is essential to strengthen the ties between citizens and their authorities. When residents are actively involved in municipal management, a sense of belonging and co-responsibility is generated, which results in better results for the community.

Social networks and digital platforms are now a link for communication and contribution between citizens and institutions. Many municipalities have implemented communication channels through social networks and web platforms to facilitate interaction with citizens. These media allow residents to express their concerns, make complaints, and follow up on municipal management.

3. Methods and materials

The research used the postulates of the positivist paradigm that led to a quantitative approach with a hypothetical deductive method, and a non-experimental cross-sectional design; the level used was correlational, for a survey with two structured questionnaires, one to measure ICT competencies and the other on citizen participation. The data were validated with a Cronbach's alpha reliability of 89.2% confidence. The tools used to analyze the information were tables, Excel, and SPSS-27 software graphics, from which descriptive and inferential data of statistical indicators were obtained.

The sample size was calculated considering a finite population of 785 students of the Faculty of Business Sciences of the National University of Huancavelica—Peru, which is composed of three schools: 256 in Economics, 264 in accounting, and 266 in administration. It is important to highlight that the student population is a relevant and key group to evaluate ICT competencies, as they are active users of technology and are in a formative stage in which they develop critical skills for citizen participation; which differs substantially from the population of the Huancavelica region whose educational condition in ICT is precarious due to their poverty condition estimated at 39.5% in 2023 according to Ref. [38].

A confidence level of 95% was established, with a critical value of 1.96, and acceptance and non-acceptance values of 0.5 were used, along with a margin of error of 5%. This resulted in an initial sample size of 254 people. Subsequently, an adjustment for finite populations was applied, leading to a final sample size of 195 students, thus ensuring the representativeness and validity of the results. Likewise, quota sampling was used to select the participants: 64 from Economics, 65 from Management, and 66 from Accounting. This process ensures that each school is represented in the sample according to its proportion within the population.

Finally, to ensure quality in data collection, methods of distributing questionnaires anonymously will be implemented to encourage honest responses; data collectors were trained for this purpose, ensuring that they fully understand the process and properly administer the surveys.

4. Results and discussion

In **Table 1**, the analysis of ICT competencies among students reveals significant differences in their levels of knowledge, skills, and attitudes. At the low level, only 1.5% of students show deficiencies in these areas, suggesting that most have access to technology and basic training, although individual or contextual barriers persist that limit their development. The vast majority (86.7% in knowledge and 73.3% in skills) are at the intermediate level, indicating functional competence in the use of technological tools for everyday tasks; however, this may imply a lack of depth in their critical understanding and confidence to participate in more complex digital citizenship initiatives. On the other hand, 11.8% of the students reach a high level of

Condition	ICT competence		D11 knowledge		D12 ability		D13 attitude	
	F	%	F	%	F	%	F	%
Low	3	1.5	5	2.6	2	1.0	3	1.5
Half	169	86.7	143	73.3	170	87.2	138	70.8
High	23	11.8	47	24.1	23	11.8	54	27.7
Total	195	100	195	100	195	100	195	100

Table 1.
Student perceptions of ICT competencies and dimensions.

competencies, suggesting that they have had additional opportunities to develop their skills, such as extracurricular courses or practical projects.

In that context, applying skills in real-life situations, as well as implementing more robust educational programs, can ensure that students are competent in using ICT effectively in their academic and professional lives.

Table 2 presents the distribution of citizen participation in four dimensions: citizen, political, social, and civic participation, among 195 students. At the low level, it is observed that 46.7% of the students qualify in the low category (91 students), while there are 45.1% in the political dimension (88 students); in the social dimension, 29.2% (57 students) and in civic, this percentage is the highest with 56.9% (111 students). The majority of students are at the medium level, with 48.7% in civic and political participation and 63.6% in social, although only 39.5% in civics. Finally, high levels are low in all dimensions, highlighting 4.6% in civic participation and 3.6% in civics.

Furthermore, the low percentages of high participation indicate that only a small group feels truly involved, which highlights the urgent need for more effective educational strategies and municipal strategies that promote not only theoretical knowledge but also motivation and opportunities to participate in political and social life.

Table 3 presents a descriptive analysis of ICT competencies and citizen participation among 195 students, showing a wide variability in the ratings. ICT competencies have an average of 81.89%, with a range from 38 to 100, indicating a positive overall level in the use of technologies. Within the specific dimensions, knowledge (D11) averages 23.74% (range 10 to 30), skills (D12) reach an average of 34.32% (range 18 to 43), and attitudes (D13) average 23.82% (range 10 to 29). As for citizen participation, the average is 59.56%, with a range that varies between 32 and 94. The political

Variables and dimensions	Citizen participation		D21 policy		D22 social		D23 civic	
	F	%	F	%	F	%	F	%
Low	91	46.7	88	45.1	57	29.2	111	56.9
Half	95	48.7	95	48.7	124	63.6	77	39.5
High	9	4.6	12	6.2	14	7.2	7	3.6
Total	195	100.0	195	100.0	195	100.0	195	100.0

Table 2.
Student perceptions on citizen participation and dimensions.

Variables and dimensions	N	Minimum	Maximum	Addition	Average	Desv.
ICT Competencies	195	38	100	15,968	81.89	8.736
D11 knowledge	195	10	30	4630	23.74	3.277
D12 skills	195	18	43	6693	34.32	4.113
D13 attitudes	195	10	29	4645	23.82	3.090
Citizen participation	195	32	94	11,614	59.56	14.464
D21 politics	195	9	33	3994	20.48	5.547
D22 social	195	10	31	3644	18.69	4.641
D23 civic	195	9	38	3976	20.39	6.458

Table 3.
Descriptive results of the variables and their dimensions.

(D21), social (D22), and civic (D23) dimensions present averages of 20.48, 18.69, and 20.39 percentage points, respectively. Together, these results allow us to identify areas where additional attention is required, as well as opportunities for specific interventions, which are essential for the formulation of future hypotheses or more in-depth studies.

To apply inferential statistical processes, the respective normality test was performed for each of the dimensions with the Kolmogorov-Smirnov statistic, which refers to the measure of the maximum difference between the empirical distribution function of the data and the normal distribution function. In this scenario, the significance (Sig.) obtained with a "p" value less than 0.05 indicates that the null hypothesis that the data come from a normal distribution can be rejected. The tests performed indicate that none of the variables follow a normal distribution, which suggests using "nonparametric tests" with the Spearman correlation statistic.

Looking at **Table 4**, regarding the inferential tests, the correlation between Citizen Participation and ICT Competence and its dimensions was analyzed, which reveals a worrying disconnection between these two fundamental aspects in the formation of active and committed citizens. Despite the growing importance of digital competences in the current context, the correlation coefficients are remarkably low and not significant, suggesting that knowledge, skills, and attitudes toward ICT are not translating into greater citizen participation. The weak negative correlation with skills and minimal positive correlations with knowledge and attitudes indicate that, although students may possess some ICT competence, this is not being reflected in real civic engagement.

Variables and dimensions	Citizen participation	ICT competencies	D11 knowledge	D12 skills	D13 attitude
Correlation coefficient	1	0.014	−0.123	0.091	0.06
Next (bilateral)		0.841	0.086	0.205	0.406
N	195	195	195	195	195

Table 4.
Spearman's rho correlations of variables and dimensions.

This finding is alarming as it raises serious questions about the effectiveness of local government educational programmers and strategies to integrate ICT learning with the promotion of active citizenship. It is imperative that these educational strategies be re-evaluated and redesigned to ensure that not only technical skills are taught, but a sense of social responsibility and active participation in the community is also fostered.

Based on this analysis, it was necessary to verify the incidence through a regression, where the ICT Competencies variable had to be excluded from the model due to presenting a high degree of multicollinearity with its dimensions, so **Table 5** was prepared to deepen the analysis.

The regression model analysis reveals that the constant is 44.290, with a high significance ($p < 0.001$), indicating a solid starting point for the model. The unstandardized coefficient for Knowledge (D11) is −1.378, suggesting that an increase in knowledge is associated with a decrease in the dependent variable, which is unexpected and could reflect a negative perception related to the acquired knowledge; this finding is highly significant ($p = 0.001$). In contrast, Skills (D12) has a positive coefficient of 1.056, indicating that an increase in skills is related to better performance or participation, and this effect is also significant ($p = 0.001$). On the other hand, the coefficient for Attitudes (D13) is 0.492, but with a significance of 0.205, suggesting that, although there is a positive effect, it is not statistically significant, raising doubts about the relevance of fostering positive attitudes toward ICT in this specific context.

Finally, we can observe that the correlations and the model present contradictory findings: while ICT Competencies are positively associated with the dependent variable, knowledge seems to have a significant negative effect, which is disconcerting and might require a deeper review of the context in which this knowledge is being applied. Furthermore, the lack of statistical significance in attitudes suggests that this dimension might need a different approach to be effectively integrated into participation strategies or training programs.

The analyzed international and national backgrounds agree that ICTs not only facilitate access to information but also expand opportunities for citizens to actively engage in public decision-making. However, it is essential to recognize that, despite the potential advantages, there are significant obstacles, such as the digital divide and the lack of training in digital skills, which can limit the real impact of these tools. Furthermore, although a growing trend toward the digitalization of citizen participation has been observed, it is crucial to question whether this digitalization really promotes more inclusive and effective governance or whether, on the contrary, it perpetuates existing inequalities by excluding those without adequate access to technology.

Model	Unstandardized coefficients		Standardized coefficients		Sig.
	B	Std. Error	Beta	t	
(Constant)	44.290	9.499		4.663	0.000
D11 knowledge	−1.378	0.399	−0.312	−3.451	0.001
D12 skills	1.056	0.326	0.300	3.237	0.001
D13 attitudes	0.492	0.387	0.105	1.272	0.205

Table 5.
Coefficients of the citizen participation variable and its relationship with the ICT Competencies variable and its dimensions.

In this context, it is vital to consider not only the development of digital platforms but also how they fit into a broader framework of civic participation and how they can be used to strengthen democratic processes. The importance of this analysis lies in its ability to inform public policies and educational strategies that seek not only to implement digital technologies but also to ensure that all citizens have the skills and opportunities necessary to participate fully in democratic life, even though the results are different in the inferential part.

5. Conclusions

The findings of the study conclude that there is a relationship between ICT Competencies and citizen participation among students of a public university in Huancavelica, Peru, based on the revelation of important facts that align with international and national literature on e-participation.

Although the background highlights the fundamental role of ICTs in enhancing civic engagement, the results obtained indicate that this relationship is not so direct. In particular, ICT knowledge is negatively associated with participation, which could indicate that greater access to information does not necessarily translate into active engagement. On the other hand, ICT Competencies show a positive correlation, suggesting that the practical development of these competencies may be a driver for greater participation. However, the low significance of attitudes raises questions about whether fostering a favorable mindset toward ICTs is enough to boost civic engagement.

This study is valid because it uses robust quantitative methods to analyze the relationship between variables, avoiding falling into spurious research that does not establish clear connections. Unlike previous studies that emphasize the importance of digital platforms as facilitators of participation, this analysis highlights the need to address other contextual factors that may influence citizen engagement. The research has significant value in offering a more nuanced understanding of how ICT Competencies can be integrated into educational strategies that truly foster active and effective participation of students in their communities. This is crucial for the development of educational policies and programs that seek not only to teach technological skills but also to empower young people as active and responsible citizens in an increasingly relevant digital environment.

The research considered that the results are spurious due to several factors that support the validity of its findings and the relationship between ICT Competencies and citizen participation. To optimize the use of statistics, clear connections were established between the variables analyzed, avoiding unfounded inferences that characterize spurious research. In addition, it is observed that ICT Competencies, especially in terms of abilities, have a positive correlation with citizen participation, which motivates a real and significant relationship. This methodological approach and the identification of significant relationships contrast with the phenomenon of spurious correlations, where variables appear related without a genuine connection.

The study also addresses a gap in the existing literature by examining how ICT Competencies do not help civic engagement, reinforcing the need for improvement in the educational field and for public management to implement easily accessible digital channels and user-friendly platforms.

In summary, the research is justified both theoretically and methodologically, providing empirical evidence that supports the relationship between the variables and contributing to the understanding of how digital competences can foster active citizenship.

Conflict of interest

The author declares that he has no conflict of interest.

Expressions of gratitude

I express my gratitude to the Editor for granting the opportunity to publish this book chapter.

Other statements

I declare that this space opens a source of inspiration and aspiration for new purposes. The roads should offer citizens active participation in decision-making in local administration policies.

Author details

Jaime Rodrigo* and Salazar Espinoza
National University of Huancavelica, Huancavelica, Peru

*Address all correspondence to: jaime.salazar@unh.edu.pe

References

[1] Naser A, Concha G. The role of ICTs in public management and planning for sustainable development in Latin America and the Caribbean. Public Management (ECLAC-UN). 2001. pp. 1-45. Available from: http://www.cepal.org/publicaciones/xml/3/52433/Rol_TIC_gestion_publica.pdf%5Cnhttp://www.eclac.cl/publicaciones/Ilpes/1/LCL1521P/lcl1521e.pdf

[2] Franciskovic J, Hamann A, Miralles F. ICT, an opportunity for citizen participation in subnational governments. Revista Republicana. 20 Jul 2020;**29**:21-46. Available from: http://ojs.urepublicana.edu.co/index.php/revistarepublicana/article/view/653/495

[3] Lu H, Fu K, Liu X, Hu W. Digital citizen participation of college students: Reality and optimization path. Problems of Education in the 21st Century. 25 Apr 2023;**81**(2):244-257. Available from: https://www.ceeol.com/search/article-detail?id=1115983

[4] Al Rashidi ME, Alalfy HR. Digital citizenship and social media impact on Saudi family cohesion: A vision 2030 perspective. International Journal of Advanced and Applied Sciences. Sep 2023;**10**(9):18-28. Available from: http://www.science-gate.com/IJAAS/2023/V10I9/1021833ijaas202309003.html

[5] Buchholz B, DeHart J, Moorman G. Digital citizenship during a global pandemic: Beyond digital literacy. Journal of Adolescent & Adult Literacy. 2020;**64**:11-17. DOI: 10.1002/jaal.1076

[6] Sorokina GP, Pershina TA, Dolgikh EA. Implementation of digital competencies in higher education educational programs in Russia. Vestnik Universiteta. 30 Jun 2022;**5**:61-70. Available from: https://vestnik.guu.ru/jour/article/view/3562

[7] Al-Zahrani A. Toward digital citizenship : Examining factors affecting participation and involvement in the internet society among higher education students. International Education Studies. 26 Nov 2015;**8**(12):203-217. Available from: http://www.ccsenet.org/journal/index.php/ies/article/view/49309

[8] Zoroayka V, Sandoval MG. Digital citizenship in higher education students. Issues in Information Systems. 2019;**20**(4):93-103. Available from: https://iacis.org/iis/2019/4_iis_2019_93-103.pdf

[9] Secinaro S, Brescia V, Iannaci D, Jonathan GM. Does citizen involvement feed on digital platforms? International Journal of Public Administration. 4 Jul 2022;**45**(9):708-725. DOI: 10.1080/01900692.2021.1887216

[10] Allen B, Tamindael LE, Bickerton SH, Cho W. Does citizen coproduction lead to better urban services in smart cities projects? An empirical study on e-participation in a mobile big data platform. Government Information Quarterly. Jan 2020;**37**(1):101412. Available from: https://linkinghub.elsevier.com/retrieve/pii/S0740624X18302302

[11] Guerrieri PM, Comai S, Fugini M. Evolving experiences of participation : Towards an e-ILAUD tool. In: 2021 IEEE International Smart Cities Conference (ISC2). Manchester, Reino Unido: IEEE; 2021. pp. 1-7. Available from: https://ieeexplore.ieee.org/document/9562887/

[12] Mutiarin D, Lawelai H. Optimizing the role of ICT and citizen participation:

Analysis of Smart City governance implementation in Jakarta, Indonesia and Kuala Lumpur, Malaysia. In: Mutiarin D, Alam M, Cahill D, Sharifuddin J, Senge M, Robani A, et al., editors. E3S Web of Conferences. Vol. 440. 2023. pp. p. 1-8, p. 03027. DOI: 10.1051/e3sconf/202344003027

[13] Shaikh AK, Baig S, Adhikari N, Al SH. E-participation system : Leveraging Blockchain technology to enhance democratic engagement. In: 2023 IEEE 8th International Conference on Engineering Technologies and Applied Sciences (ICETAS). IEEE; 2023. pp. 1-5. Available from: https://ieeexplore.ieee.org/document/10346551/

[14] Adam IO, Dzang AM. The mediating role of ICT regulation on the effects of ICT access and ICT use on e-participation : Evidence from structural equation modelling and necessary condition analysis. African Journal of Science, Technology, Innovation and Development. 2022;**14**(5):1161-1172. DOI: 10.1080/20421338.2021.1937815

[15] Santamaria-Philco A, Quiroz-Palma P, Herrera-Tapia J, Macias-Mendoza D, Munoz-Verduga D, Sendon-Varela J. E-participation tool for decision support based on the ePfw framework. In: 2022 17th Iberian Conference on Information Systems and Technologies (CISTI). IEEE; 2022. pp. 1-6. Available from: https://ieeexplore.ieee.org/document/9820351/

[16] Olawoyin KW. X-raying citizenship participation through the lens of ICT: Quest for democratic governance and development in Nigeria. Study Policy Slovakia. 2023;**XV**(2). Available from: http://www.sps.sav.sk/x-raying-citizenship-participation-through-the-lens-of-ict-quest-for-democratic-governance-and-development-in-nigeria/

[17] Lee DS, Kwon GH, Moon SH. The influence of perceived risk on online citizen participation. The Korean Association of Governance Studies. 2022;**32**(2):163-185. Available from: https://scholar.kyobobook.co.kr/article/detail/4010036745514

[18] Okwudibe EO, Adomi EE. Relationship between ICT skills and participation in zoom meetings for professional development among librarians in universities in south-south, Nigeria. Journal of Management and Social Science Research. 2023;**4**(1):40-49. Available from: https://credencepressltd.com/journal/uploads/archive/20231693231782856628531 8.pdf

[19] Cabero-Almenara J, Palacios-Rodríguez A. European framework for digital competence for teachers «DigCompEdu». Translation and adaptation of the «DigCompEdu» questionnaire check-in. EDMETIC. 2020;**9**(1):213-234. Available from: https://www.uco.es/ucopress/ojs/index.php/edmetic/article/view/12462

[20] Hernández Suárez CA. ICT competencies for the professional development of teachers in basic education. Praxis & Saber. 2016;**7**(14):41. Available from: http://revistas.uptc.edu.co/revistas/index.php/praxis_saber/article/view/5217

[21] Arras Vota AM d G, Torres-Gastelú CA, García Valcárcel Muñoz Repiso A. Information and communication technology (ICT) competencies of university students. Latin American Journal of Social Communication. 2022;**66**:337-359. Available from: https://nuevaepoca.revistalatinacs.org/index.php/revista/article/view/1064

[22] Vera A, Rivas A. Monitoring Digital Education Policies in Latin

America and the Caribbean. UNESCO IIEP Office for Latin America and the Caribbean; 2023. p. 9. Available from: https://unesdoc.unesco.org/ark:/48223/pf0000386982

[23] UNESCO. Advancing Mobily literacy in Bangladesh. In: Guidebook. UNESCO; 2018. p. 29. Available from: https://unesdoc.unesco.org/ark:/48223/pf0000372983

[24] European Commission, Joint Research Centre, Vuorikari R, Kluzer S, Punie Y. DigComp 2.2, the Digital Competence Framework for Citizens—With New Examples of Knowledge, Skills and Attitudes. Publications Office of the European Union; 2022. Available from: https://publications.jrc.ec.europa.eu/repository/handle/JRC128415

[25] Kumar N, Vragov R. Active citizen participation using ICT tools. Communications of the ACM. 2009;**52**(1):118-121. DOI: 10.1145/1435417.1435444

[26] Loukis E, Charalabidis Y, Millard J. From the special issue editors: European research on electronic citizen participation and engagement in public policy making. Information Systems Management. 2012;**29**(4):255-257. DOI: 10.1080/10580530.2012.716738

[27] Alarabiat A. Electronic participation through social media. In: Proceedings of the 9th International Conference on Theory and Practice of Electronic Governance. New York, NY, USA: ACM; 2016. pp. 424-427. DOI: 10.1145/2910019.2910090

[28] Boudjelida A, Mellouli S. A multidimensional analysis approach for electronic citizens participation. In: Proceedings of the 17th International Digital Government Research Conference on Digital Government Research. New York, NY, USA: ACM; 2016. pp. 49-57. DOI: 10.1145/2912160.2912195

[29] Musiał-Karg M, Kapsa I. In: Saltador C, editor. Attitudes of Polish Voters Towards Introduction of e-Voting in the Context of Political Factors. 2020. pp. 144-160. DOI: 10.1007/978-3-030-37545-4_10

[30] Zheng Y. Explaining citizens' e-participation usage. Administration and Society. 2017;**49**(3):423-442. DOI: 10.1177/0095399715593313

[31] Barber B. In: Barber BR, editor. Strong Democracy. University of California Press; 2004. DOI: 10.1525/9780520351912/html

[32] Huh T, Kim JH. Multiple Conjunctural impact on digital social innovation: Focusing on the OECD countries. Sustainability. 2019;**11**(18):4887. Available from: https://www.mdpi.com/2071-1050/11/18/4887

[33] Marzouki A, Mellouli S, Daniel S. Towards a context-based citizen participation approach. In: Proceedings of the 10th International Conference on Theory and Practice of Electronic Governance. New York, NY, USA: ACM; 2017. pp. 204-213. DOI: 10.1145/3047273.3047352

[34] Woodward R. The organization for economic cooperation and development. New Political Economy. 2004;**9**(1):113-127. DOI: 10.1080/1356346042000190411

[35] Congress of the Republic. Constitution Politics of Peru. Government of Peru; 1993. pp. 117-125. Available from: https://lpderecho.pe/constitucion-politica-peru-actualizada/

[36] Congress of the Republic of Peru. Law No. 26300—Law on the Rights of Citizen

Participation and Control. Official Gazette El Peruano; 1994. p. 5. Available from: https://www.leyes.congreso.gob.pe/DetLeyNume_1p.aspx?xNorma=6&xNumero=26300&xTipoNorma=0

[37] Congress of the Republic of Peru. Law 27972—Organic Law of Municipalities2003. pp. 244876-244900. Available from: https://www.leyes.congreso.gob.pe/DetLeyNume_1p.aspx?xNorma=6&xNumero=27972&xTipoNorma=0

[38] INEI (Instituto Nacional de Estadística). National Household Survey 2014-2033. 2023. Available from: https://www.gob.pe/institucion/inei/colecciones/21871-condiciones-de-vida-y-pobreza